Praise for _Brigit: Sun of Womanhood_

"_Bright: Sun of Womanhood_ is an encyclopedic compendium of various aspects of the female spirit. Rather than being a daunting read, it is a delight from beginning to end. There is something for everyone—male and female alike—within these pages, from the casual reader who is simply looking for light entertainment to the empathetic scholar seeking to broaden an already wide base of esoteric knowledge. The authors wisely have laid down no dictum of beliefs. There is no dogma; no hard and fast perimeter. The book is as transparent and full of joy as the spirit it celebrates, yet it also offers a serious, thought-provoking journey that will leave no pilgrim unmoved."

—Morgan Llywelyn
Lion of Ireland and Druids

"This anthology is a deeply intelligent, wise, and alluring immersion into the living presence of Brigit, a creation of ritual space that is both ancient and immediate."

—Charlene Spretnak
Lost Goddesses of Early Greece

"This wonderful collection of essays, poems, reflections, meditations and scholarship brilliantly captures the complexity, richness, and fertility of Brigit's traditions. For many disenfranchised by male separatist religions, Brigit's traditions allow us to hear ourselves think, and to hear each other into speech in thealogical mode. This volume will further spread Brigit's cloak around the world, wrapping her followers in the comfort of her compassion, and inspiring them to weave their own cloaks, nurturing them as they protect our vulnerable planet, Earth."

—Mary Condren
The Serpent and the Goddess: Women, Religion and
Power in Celtic Ireland, and a forthcoming major study on Brigit,
the Cailleach or Wise Woman of Ancient Ireland.

"*Brigit, Sun of Womanhood*, edited by Michael McDermott and Patricia Monaghan, is a comprehensive and compelling collection of fiction, poetry, essays, and photographs that celebrate Brigit in all Her many manifestations as ancient Goddess, legendary Catholic abbess and saint, and modern-day archetype of the divine female. The stories shared in this anthology will delight and inform, whether or not one's ethnicity is rooted in Celtic traditions. Like the color-drenched prisms of a finely crafted kaleidoscope, this book opens the reader's eyes and heart to the magical, multi-faceted aspects of this Goddess's legacy and the potent medicine She offers. Informative and entertaining, this anthology serves up a soul-quenching helping of milk and fire, poetry and ritual that's sure to satisfy contemporary seekers."

—**Mary Saracino**
co-editor of *She Is Everywhere! Volume 3: An Anthology of Writings in Womanist/Feminist Spirituality (iUniverse 2012)* and author of the novel, *The Singing of Swans* (Pearlsong Press 2006). For more information visit: www.marysaracino.com

BRIGIT:
SUN OF WOMANHOOD

Edited by
Patricia Monaghan and
Michael McDermott

Printed in the United States of America
ISBN: 978-0-9833466-3-0

Published by
Goddess Ink, Ltd., Las Vegas, Nevada
www.goddess-ink.com

Designed by Soujanya Rao
Front cover artwork by Katlyn Breene
Back cover art by Eric Koenig
Interior artwork by Katlyn Breene (www.mermadearts.com)

A portion of the proceeds from this volume go to support the work of Solas Bhríde, the
Christian and Celtic spirituality center founded by the Brigidine Sisters in Kildare,
Ireland. They are currently building an eco-center and hermitage dedicated to Saint
Bridget, near the famous wells dedicated to her. Solas Bhríde sponsors an Imbolc festival
each year that draws hundreds of devotees to Kildare and to the holy wells.
www.solasbhride.ie

Excerpt from Magliocco, Sabina. *Witching Culture: Folklore and Neopaganism in
America*. State College: University of Pennsylvania Press, 2004, pp. 1–3. Used by
permission of University of Pennsylvania Press.

Excerpt from Cunningham, Elizabeth. *Magdalen Rising*. Rhinebeck, New York:
Monkfish Press, 2007. From chapter 37, "Caught in the Web of Life," pp. 317–322.
Used by permission of Monkfish Press.

Excerpt from Webster, Cindy. *Brigid of Ireland*. London: Monarch Books, an imprint of
Lion Hudson. Used by permission of Monarch Books.

Excerpt from Minihan, Rita, from the out-of-print pamphlet, *Re-kindling the Flame*.
Used by permission of the author.

The first part of Carol P. Christ's essay was presented at Brigid's Place, Christ Church
Cathedral in Houston, Texas in 2004 and published in somewhat different form in
Women's Journal 11/1 (Spring 2004), pp. 13–14. The concluding stories of that essay
were published in somewhat different form on the *Alive Mind and Spirit* blog in 2008.

To Brigit

CONTENTS

BRIGIT, GODDESS OF THE CELTS

SAINT BRIGIT

BRIGIT IN THE TWENTY-FIRST CENTURY

SONG TO BRIGIT

Traditional, adapted by Patricia Monaghan

Brigit, red-gold woman,
Brigit, flame and honeycomb,
Brigit, sun of womanhood,
Brigit, lead me home.

You are a branch in blossom.
You are a sheltering dome.
You are my bright blessed freedom.
Brigit, lead me home.

INTRODUCTION

Michael McDermott and Patricia Monaghan

Throughout the world, for the last two decades or more, we have seen a revival of interest in the figure of Brigit. In Ireland, where this revival is especially strong, Saint Bridget is honored by Christians (both Catholic and Protestant), who often celebrate her in company with spiritual seekers who identify more closely with the pre-Christian Brigit. In other areas of the world—including America, Scotland, Cornwall, Wales, Scandinavia, and even the Caribbean, and among Christians, Pagans, practitioners of diaspora religions, and many others—Brigit holds a special place. Brigit extends her call both as goddess and saint.

We are honored to edit this anthology about Brigit: ancient goddess, legendary saint, and abbess. She gives solace to those who pray to her and has a special connection in history to those looking for figures and beliefs from ancient times. Other images help to make these connections: Our Lady of Guadalupe, connected to the Aztec goddess Tonan, fulfills this role for those of Latin American heritage; African deities stand this way for the slave-determined diaspora; Greek, Roman, or Scandinavian deities are sought for heritage or aesthetic reasons. Brigit is serving those who seek these ancient ties as well, whether they identify with Celtic culture through heritage or through other interests.

We have both been involved with Brigit for many years. As Irish-Americans who were raised Catholic and who now describe them-selves as post-Christian pre-Christians, we experience Brigit playing a role that answers many spiritual questions. We have each pursued a path of seeking knowledge about Brigit and making her a central part of our lives. The land in the Driftless area of Wisconsin where we live, which resembles some areas of Ireland that we know well, is dedicated to her and is named Brigit Rest. The twenty acres of Brigit Rest is growing into a center for Celtic spirituality and is the base for the Black Earth Institute, a progressive think-tank connecting artists whose work celebrates the intersection of spirituality, ecology, and social justice.

The continuity between the goddess and the saint is unbreakable. She is a bridge in many ways between Christians and Pagans, between Catholics and Protestants in Ireland, even between Northern Europeans and descendants of African slaves in the Caribbean. She encompasses all these realities. This anthology grew from the awareness of Brigit's increasing importance to both men and women seeking a holistic, embracing spirituality.

This collection of fiction, poetry, and essays is divided into three sections: the first discusses Brigit as goddess; the second concentrates on her appearance as Christian saint; and the third explores the multiple ways she appears in today's culture. We hope that there is something to satisfy everyone and something to provoke everyone to further thought about this important figure in world religions.

Notes on the Text

Irish is not English. Scots Gaelic is not English. The languages were not originally written, as the Celtic peoples had (and, some argue, still have) oral cultures. When these languages came to be transliterated into English, various spellings of Brigit emerged, of which Brighid was the early-modern version, later changed to Brigit or Brigid, although the modern Irish spelling is Bríd, with the accent mark indicating that the pronunciation is rather like the English word "breed." In Scots Gaelic, the name is Brìghde or Brìde, while other Anglicized forms include Bridey or Bridie and Breeda, as well as the common Bridget. In Welsh, because of consonant shifts, the name becomes Ffraid or Fraid. Whether or not the figure is the same as the goddesses found among British and continental Celts as Brigantia or Brigandu is not fully established.

However, an amazing diversity of spellings appear in various books and articles, including Brighit, Brigitte, Bhrigit, Brighet, Bridhe, and so forth. Some are older, now-outdated spellings, while others indicate an attempt to make the spelling look Irish or Gaelic without fully under-standing transliteration rules. For the purposes of this book, we have selected the common Irish spelling of Brigit for the goddess, and Bridget for the saint, so that they may be distinguished when necessary. Where one of the figures from an area outside Ireland or the Irish diaspora is discussed, the appropriate spelling is used. The exceptions are in citations, where the original spelling of the author is used, and in excerpts from novels, where the spelling remains as in the original text.

Another area of divergence in various texts has to do with the date of Imbolc, the feast of Brigit. This appears variously as February 1 and

February 2, although occasionally a writer will refer to it occurring on January 31. At base, this confusion comes because the ancient Celts marked the beginning of a "day" as what we would consider the previous evening. Thus Hallowe'en or Samhain, November 1, would begin on October 31, the "evening" or "e'en" of the previous day. In the same way, Imbolc began at sundown on January 31 and extended through the next day. The Roman Catholic Church, which often adopted and adapted earlier religious holidays, chose February 2 for the feast of Candlemas—the feast of the purification of the Virgin Mary in the temple after the birth of Jesus. On that day, candles were blessed for the following day's feast of Saint Blaise, patron of throat diseases. Contemporary American Neopagans often celebrate Imbolc on February 2 (though some celebrate on February 3 or 4, the astronomical midpoint between the winter solstice and the vernal equinox), but the tradition that Saint Bridget's day is February 1 (and the previous evening) is firmly held in Ireland and other lands of the Celtic fringe.

BRIGIT
GODDESS OF THE CELTS

Brigit, Sacred Virginity, and the Elements of Perpetual Energy

Miriam Robbins Dexter

The pagan Irish triple goddess Brigit, the daughter of the Dagda (the shining god of the heavens), was patroness of poets, smith-goddess, and goddess of healing. In pagan Ireland, she had a son, Ruadan; that is, early on, she was not a virgin, as she became later under Christianity. When she was assimilated into Celtic Christianity, she regained her virginity, becoming a virgin nun. According to Geraldus Cambrensis, writing from approximately 1146 to 1220 CE in "De Igne A Brigida Sua Nocte Servato," she and her attendant nuns guarded a perpetual flame:

> At the time of Brigit
> twenty nuns here served a master as would a soldier,
> she herself being the twentieth . . .
> when indeed every night through every succession
> they cared for the fire . . .
> on the twentieth night the last nun
> said: 'Brigit, I have cared for your fire
> and thus, the fire having been left . . .
> it was found again,
> unextinguished.'

> *Cum tempore Brigide xx moniales hic Domino militassent, ipsa*
> *vicesima existente. . . . Cum vero singulis noctibus singule per*
> *ordinem ignem custodiant, nocte vicesima monialis ultima . . .*

inquit: Brigida, custodi ignem tuum. Et sic, igne relicto . . .
inextinctus reperitur. *

Not only was Brigit significant in the element of fire; she was associated with the element of water as well. Her name was given to holy
wells and to several rivers, including the Brighid in Ireland, the Braint
in Wales, and the Brent in England. As a virgin, Brigit embodied a
most potent form of energy in its stored form; her energies were held in
reserve, just as a battery stores energy. This is a different sort of energy
from that of a woman who gives energy sexually, as I argued in my 1990
book, *Whence the Goddesses*. The forces of these elements are perpetual:
water can flow infinitely, just as fire can burn continuously. A virgin such
as Bridget the nun was replete with the stores of energy that might guar-
antee the perpetuity of both elements.

Through the past two millennia, Brigit has remained important to
the people of Ireland and beyond. Her feast day, February 1, also called
Imbolc, is celebrated worldwide. Her perpetual flame in Kildare was kept
unextinguished until the 16th century, and it was relit by the Brigidine
Sisters in 1993. It became a perpetual flame again in 2006 and it still
burns.

Another name for Brigit is Saint Bride; Saint Bride's Day is still
celebrated, and hymns, such as the following 20th century song found in
the Scottish region of Ross, are sung to her:

Early on Bride's morn
The serpent shall come from the hole;
I will not molest the serpent,
nor will the serpent molest me . . .

This is the Day of Bride.
The queen will come from the mound;
I will not touch the queen,
nor will the queen touch me.

---

* Editor's Note: All translations by the author.

In this poem we see that Brigit is associated with the female serpent, called the "queen," similar to the Indic Nirṛti, who was Sarparajnī (literally, "the Queen of Serpents" in *Śatapatha Brāhmaṇa*). This female serpent is beneficent; it is not feared because it does not molest the devotee. Brigit's roots, indeed, extend back to the European Neolithic snake goddess who, as Marija Gimbutas amply demonstrated, was depicted in figurines from the 6th through the 3rd millennia BCE.

The concept of the sacred fire, and sometimes its association with virginity, is found in several Indo-European cultures, among which are those of Ireland, Greece, Rome, and Lithuania. The Greek goddess Hestia was the personification of the pure core of the home: the hearth. She was required to be a virgin, as we learn in the *Homeric Hymn* to Aphrodite written sometime between the 8th to 6th centuries BCE:

> Nor yet are Aphrodite's works
> for the venerable virgin, Hestia . . .
> she swore a mighty oath . . .
> that she would be a virgin all of her days. . . .

> οὐδὲ μὲν αἰδοίη κούρη ἅδε ἔργ᾽ Ἀφροδίτης, / Ἱστίη . . . ὤμοσε δὲ
> μέγαν ὅρκον . . . / παρθένος ἔσσεσθαι πάντ᾽ ἤματα . . .

In Greece, the priestesses of the hearth goddess could be any age, and they need not be virgins, although they were required to be celibate. The sacred fire could even be maintained by an elderly married woman, as long as she no longer cohabited with her husband. Such was the case with the Pythia at Delphi.

Vesta, the Roman equivalent of Hestia, was also a virgin. She was the third daughter of Ops (goddess of abundance) and Saturn (god of time). Ovid, in the Fasti, tells us this of her:

> The others married. . . . of the three one resisted,
> refusing to endure a husband. . . .
> Do not perceive Vesta as anything but the living flame,
> and you see that no bodies are born of flame.

Therefore, she is justly a virgin who neither sends forth nor takes seeds, and she loves companions [the Vestal Virgins] in her virginity.

Utraque nupserunt. . . . de tribus impatiens restitit una viri. . . . nec tu aliud Vestam quam vivam intellege flammam, nataque de flamma corpora nulla vides. Iure igitur virgo est, quae semina nulla remittit nec capit et comites virginitatis amat.

Vesta's attendants were required to be literal virgins, in contrast to the priestesses of Hestia. These priestesses were called the Vestal Virgins: the virgins of Vesta. They were politically very important priestesses of the hearth, and they performed various rituals to benefit the Roman state. If any Vestal were to violate the rule of chastity, it is said that her punishment would be live inhumation, as we again learn from the *Fasti* of Ovid:

> . . . nor will it be said
> that under [the emperor's] leadership
> any priestess violated her sacred fillets,
> and none shall be buried alive in the ground.
> It is thus that an unchaste [Vestal] perishes,
> because that [earth] which she violated,
> in that [earth] she is interred;
> and indeed Earth and Vesta are the same deity.

Nullaque dicitur vittas temerasse sacerdos hoc duce nec viva defodietur humo. Sic incesta petit, quia quam violavit, in illam conditur, et Tellus Vestaque numen idem.

It was necessary to the Roman state for the Roman Vestals to remain virgins, because only through virginity could their sacred energy have been saved for their office rather than dissipated through the sexual act. Further, if a woman was neither virgin nor married, she became a threat to the patriarchal, patrilineal Roman establishment, since if she was both unmarried (un-ruled by a husband) and sexual, she was thus autonomous.

Any woman who took control of her own sexuality, in Rome as elsewhere, was both condemned and feared by those societies.

It is significant that any maiden, no matter what social class she
belonged to, was eligible to become a Vestal Virgin. Nor need she be
young. In 19 CE, Tacitus, in his *Annals*, tells us that the Roman emperor
Tiberius:

> proposed the selection of a virgin in place of Occia,
> who had presided over the Vestal rites with the greatest purity
> for fifty-seven years.

> *Rettulit . . . capiendam virginem in locum Occiae, quae septem et*
> *quinquaginta per annos summa sanctimonia*
> *Vestalibus sacris praesederat.*

The sacred power was present in all Roman women.

The Balts had religious fire rituals similar to those of the Romans
and Celts. A perpetual flame, sacred to the thunder god, Perkunas,
was tended, as the 18th century scholar S. Rostowski recorded (and
Mannhardt republished a hundred years later):

> For Perkunas they used to maintain a perpetual sacred fire,
> in the woods, imitating Roman Vestals.

> *Perkuno ignem in sylvis sacrum, vestales Romanas imitati,*
> *perpetuum alebant.*

This flame was guarded by priests and priestesses, called *vaidelotai*
or *vaidelutes*. Further, unmarried female vaidelutes served Potrimpus (a
god of rivers and springs), or his snake-epiphany, with a nonperpetual
fire and with milk.

The juxtaposition of fire, waters, and snakes provides a striking parallel to the Celtic honoring of the goddess and nun, Brigit. Thus Brigit, who
in origin was a powerful triple goddess—perhaps a pre-Indo-European
great goddess of Ireland—became both Indo-Europeanized and

Christianized; so it was that she gave her energies to the task of maintaining both fire and water in perpetuity for the people of Ireland.

REFERENCES:

Allen, T. W., W. R. Halliday, and E. E. Sikes, eds. 1980. *The Homeric Hymns*. Amsterdam: A. M. Hakkert.

Cambrensis, Geraldus. N.D. "Giraldus Cambrensis in Topographia Hibernie." In R*oyal Irish Academy Proceedings 1949* 52 C 4. Edited by John O'Meara, 1949. Dublin: Hodges, Figgis & Co.

Dexter, Miriam Robbins. 1990. *Whence the Goddesses: A Source Book*. New York: Pergamon. (Teachers College, Athene Series.)

Gimbutas, Marija. 1974. *The Gods and Goddesses of Old Europe, 6500–3500 BC: Myths and Cult Images*. Los Angeles: University of California Press.

—1989. *The Language of the Goddess*. San Francisco: HarperSanFrancisco.

—1999. *The Living Goddesses*. Edited and supplemented by Miriam Robbins Dexter. Berkeley/Los Angeles: University of California Press.

Haase, Friedrich. 1855. *Cornelii Taciti Opera*. Edited by Cornelius Tacitus. Lipsiae: Tauchnitz.

Mannhardt, Wilhelm. 1936. *Letto-Preussische Götterlehre*. Riga: Lettisch-Literärische Gesellschaft.

Merkel, R., ed. 1907. *Ovid: Works*. Leipzig: Teubner.

Ross, Anne. 1976. *The Folklore of the Scottish Highlands*. London: Batsford.

BRIGIT'S LITANY

Barbara Flaherty

Bride of the Waters, Brigit of the Air
Begoibne of the Fire, Brighid of the Earth,
Breo-saight of the Spirit, be with us.

Lady of the Hearth Fire, Lady of the Forge Fire,
Lady of Wisdom and Inspiration,
Fiery Arrow of Knowledge, be with us.

Mary of the Gael, Mother of Compassion,
Nurse of Christ, Foster-mother of Christ,
Protectress in Childbirth, be with us.

Daughter of the Druid, Bishop of Kildare,
Guardian of Indigenous Wisdom, Mother of Monastic Fire,
Mother of Memory, be with us.

Lady of the Flowing Sea, Lady of the Calm Heart,
the Soft Palm, Well of Healing, Strength of the New Moon.
Lady whose feet walk with respect upon the land, be with us.

Brigit of the Peat-heap, Brigit of the Fields,
Brigit of the Sea and Rocky Summits,
Guardian of the Children of the Land, be with us.

Brigit of the crane, swan, deer, wolf, horse, and hound.
Protectress of the flocks, herds, and fields,
Spring of the year, Feast of New Milk, be with us.

Whispering voice in the ear of poets,
healers, blacksmiths, Mother of All Crafts,
Brigit of the Mantles, be with us.

Mistress of Seeing, Lady of Healing,
Lady of the Mirror, Woman of the Spindle,
Lady of Augury, Lady of the Cauldron, be with us.

Holy are your wells and springs,
your groves and barrows, hearth fire, and forge.
Mother, teach us again and again, be with us.

The Great Bear Mother: A Journey with Brigit to the Ancient Dawn of Imbolc

Jude Lally

My sense of Brigit has always been timeless, her roots stretching back past saint and Celtic goddess. This idea began to take form when I encountered the work of Irish scholar Séamus Ó Catháin, suggesting that Brigit was the great bear mother, venerated in early bear cults. Alongside this interest lay a question: "Does the source of the new consciousness required by our modern world lay in an ancient spirituality?" This journey took me to the earliest Imbolc, to the bear emerging from hibernation: a symbol of renewal, sacrifice, and ritual. Coded themes within myth revealed a very different Imbolc from the one of the Celts—familiar motifs representing something hidden, taboo, whose roots stretch back to a far older time.

The theme of regeneration emerges throughout, and employing Joanna Macy's work in examining our modern sense of self expands who we are when we consider our ecological self. Brigit reminds us of our creativity, our ability to remember, revision, and reclaim, as if she herself morphs and changes to meet our needs.

In his seminal book, *The Festival of Brigid: Celtic Goddess and Holy Woman*, Ó Catháin suggests that the folklore associated with Brighid shows a continuous link stretching back to shamanic practice 4,000 years ago to early bear cults. The stories he searched within Nordic, Celtic, and Germanic folklore hold the same knowledge, which exists within the layers of our unconscious as ancient folk memory. The bear wasn't just a biological entity to our ancestors; Shephard, Sanders, and Snyder contend that she represented both the physical and magical qualities early bear worshipers observed. She was a wise teacher, a loving mother who was fiercely protective of her young. Each fall, ancient peoples observed the bear going into hibernation, and in the heart of winter she would have appeared dead, her heartbeat slow and her breathing barely noticeable. To observe the same bear coming back from the dead would suggest magical powers, that she was a communicator with the otherworld.

Emerging from the dead, bearing new life in the form of cubs, she also emerged bearing life to the land itself. She breathed life into the dead of winter, which lost its grip as the stirrings of spring radiated throughout the soil. All of these qualities fed our ancestors' spiritual beliefs, creating myths, ritual, and practices to live by, which also marked the great cycle of the seasons.

Marija Gimbutas, in her archaeological work, unearthed what may be evidence of bear cults in the form of figurines, possibly representing the bear as birth goddess. Small figurines from Eastern Europe 5,000 BCE have been discovered and called "bear nurses," which depict human figures wearing bear masks. Similarly, we find "bear madonna" figures dating from 6,000 BCE that depict human female figurines wearing a bear mask while holding a bear cub. The existence of such ancient figures shows the importance and variation of the image. The idea of the bear cult, however, has flourished in popular culture, quite possibly owing its success to evoking our ancient memory.

Gimbutas offers linguistic evidence to illustrate the connection of the bear with birth. The Proto Indo-European root *bhere* refers both to the bear and also to the ability to give birth. This is reflected in the Germanic *beran* (to bear children or to carry) and the Germanic *barnam* (child), as well as being present in the Old Norse *burdh* (birth.)

Circumpolar societies associate the bear with supernatural qualities, although this similarity of beliefs is not related to a common ancestral belief system, but one that each culture developed separately due to revering the bear above all other creatures. From ancient Siberia, Shepard et al illustrate a practice of sacrificing a male bear, which was seen as essential in maintaining the order of the shamanic worlds. Within early myths, Ó Catháin notes the symbolism of shamans using the psychedelic mushroom *Amanita muscaria* (fly agaric, which he color codes as "white speckled"), linking its use to rituals undertaken at Imbolc. McIntosh speculates that Imbolc could have been an ancient magic mushroom festival celebrating the essence of spring with the new life as it dawns, radiating out across face of the northern hemisphere.

A. muscaria use was likely at this cycle of the year to facilitate communication with the otherworld, ensuring the return of spring to the land and the survival of life. Laurie and White highlight one reason why the role of psychoactive mushrooms in Celtic mythology has been overlooked: with the demise of the old growth forests in Ireland, *A. muscaria* is rare in the Ireland of today. While it is likely that it grew in such forests, dried *A muscaria* could have been easily obtained from the *filidh's* (poet-seer's) Celtic neighbors.

While *A. muscaria* use is documented in numerous cultures throughout Europe and Asia, there are only obscure references to it within Celtic culture. Celtic legends are full of sleep-inducing berries and apples as well as magical hazelnuts and salmon. These were selected by the *filidh* as magical foods, yet there is nothing psychotropic about the foods that would allow them to produce inspiring and prophetic visions. The Roman historian Laertius recorded that Celtic Druids and bards spoke in "riddles and dark sayings," and it seems many taboo subjects were referenced in obscure and coded ways. Motifs of such magical foods could be explained as being metaphoric references to *A. muscaria*, as it is probable that direct referencing was taboo due to its sacred qualities, argue Laurie and White.

Inspiration and divination was fundamental to the *filidh*, and Brigit, as patron of poets, would have been invoked in rituals undertaken to inspire ecstatic poetry and induce prophetic visions. Brigit was a fire goddess, and instances throughout her life associated with pillars of flames around her head could have been an ancient coding for *A. muscaria*, which produces a pronounced heating of the head.

While possible *A. muscaria* references were coded, so too were Brigit's associations with speckled cow and snake, both having otherworldly origins. Her association with the snake is well known, and Scottish and Irish folk references refer to *A. muscaria* as the speckled snake. There is a possible link to Saint Patrick who, in banning certain pagan rituals as well as banishing snakes from Ireland, was actually attempting to wipe out an *A. muscari* cult, claim Laurie and White.

Later agricultural communities celebrated Imbolc as a time when Brigit brought the new life to the land; with milk being so important to the Celtic diet, the celebration also anticipated the lactation of the pregnant ewes. Ó Catháin notes that, when anyone complained of the depleted winter's store, they were met by reassurances that, "it won't be scarce very long now as Saint Bridget and her white cow will be coming 'round soon."

With the loss of such rich mythology, our sense of self has undergone a shrinking; once capable of shape-shifting, that self is now reduced to a mere shadow. Statistics abound with graphs showing sharp rises in the use of antidepressants alongside our insatiable hunger for consumerism. This, in part, explains our reaction to an unconscious feeling of loss, partly due to the urgency of the overwhelming array of issues vying for our attention.

The root of this great change lies in the destruction of tribal Europe and the worship of the great goddess, where our sense of self was drawn from each other, our non-human family, and the land. Salomonsen explains that these early matrifocal and matrilineal cultures, which laid down the foundation for our civilization, were eventually conquered by worshipers of a male warrior god, which lay the foundation for patriarchal and oppressive societies in Europe. The overthrow of the goddess by a male god, whose reign is removed from the earth, brought about an epic change in thought, which is still in place and dominates cultural thinking that places women, animals, and the earth as second-class citizens. As we adapted to this new myth, our notion of self changed. The founding principle of the myth of progress is self-destruction. It views our race as apart and separate from nature, concerned only with economic growth and material accumulation.

In Celtic culture, it was the role of the bard, devoted to Brigit, who kept the myths—the stories of the people—alive. McIntosh explains that this poetic power was eroded away by repressive laws such as the 1609 Statutes of Iona in the Highlands of Scotland, which suppressed Gaelic culture. Clan chiefs were required to send their eldest son or daughter south to learn English. Bards were outlawed and chiefs were no longer allowed to entertain them, with the threat of being punished or banished.

Similar laws were replicated throughout the ancient Celtic world, repressing the bard's role in maintaining cultural and ecological awareness, and were replaced by the power of money and the adoption of values of commerce. The crisis currently unfolding on our planet is a spiritual one whose roots stem from a dysfunctional and pathological notion of the self. Could the loss of the bear, in Scotland and Ireland—the loss of ancient forests, of habitat, of indigenous belief—be the reason for the shrinking of our notion of self? With each loss, we are losing aspects of ourselves.

Joanna Macy's work centers around accepting the pain we feel in facing the overwhelming issues in our current world, before it develops into grief and denial, so we are able to turn our feelings into effective action. In defining ourselves, we naturally adopt different notions of self to meet different needs. While we are free to select our boundaries—whether they end at our skin, our family, our tribe, our non-human family, the mountains, the oceans, the planet, ancient goddesses and gods, or they extend to the very universe—Macy envisions that a return to this ecological self will bring us into kinship with other forms of life, and ultimately bring us new reserves of strength.

Reconnecting is one route to wholeness, to reassembling our missing parts. The method employed does not lie outside; instead, it is a journey inwards, deep into our bones, our blood, our cells, our DNA, where remnants of ancient memory have been passed down through the generations. This was my journey in rediscovering Brigit, resonating with her as bear mother. Myths are the language of the soul, and the essence of a myth only comes alive when it resonates in the soul of the recipient. Just because the bear no longer roams in the Celtic lands of Scotland and Ireland, this does not mean that the same psychological needs that brought about the veneration of the bear are no longer relevant.

As Brigit regenerated the land, her regenerated spirit becomes meaningful again. She offers us the inspiration to envision a future which values our nonhuman relatives and the earth in our natural relationship of interconnection. Rather than accepting a future borne out of fear and helplessness featured in films that feed us horrors of ecological destruction, we must join in creating an empowering vision in which technology serves us in renewable ways, and empowers us to create sustainable futures right now. Brigit spans the existence of humankind, offering the deep well of wisdom to those who seek her. In rediscovering her symbols, hidden in layers of myth and accumulated in tales told over the years, her symbols, which might at first seem obscure, produce a powerful picture once they are reassembled.

Brigit is the great mother bear who returns the energy to the land after winter. As she regenerates the land, her regenerated spirit becomes meaningful again. She is the great mother who midwives our continual rebirth, her flame the transforming fire that burns within us. She is the fire of inspiration that the Druid *filidh* invoked, the fire that ignites our heads to dream new dreams, burns in our heart as compassion, and warms our hands in the work we carry out.

REFERENCES:

Condren, M. T. 2002. "Brigid: Soulsmith in the New Millennium." *Irish Journal of Feminist Studies* 4 (2): 34–39. Cork, Ireland: University Press.

Gimbutas, M. 2001. *The Language of the Goddess*. London: Thames & Hudson.

Laurie, E. R., and T. White. 1997. "Speckled Snake, Brother of Birch: *Amanita Muscaria* Motifs in Celtic Legends." *Shaman's Drum* 44.

McIntosh, A. 1998. "Deep Ecology and the Last Wolf." *United Nations Biodiversity Proceedings: Cultural and Spiritual Values of Biodiversity*. Cambridge: Cambridge University Press.

Macy, Joanna. 2007. *World as Lover, World as Self: Courage for Global Justice and Ecological Renewal*. Berkeley, CA: Parallex Press.

Ó Cathain, Seamus. 1995. *The Festival of Brigid: Celtic Goddess and Holy Woman*. Ireland: DBA Publications.

Shepard, Paul, Barry Sanders, and Gary Snyder. 1992. *The Sacred Paw: The Bear in Nature, Myth and Literature*. New York: Viking Press.

Invocation to Brigit

Ruth Barrett

Bright Arrow soaring,
flowing through the air
like your healing waters,
from womb flower spilling
to bathe the weak, the sorrowful, the forgotten.
Compassionate healer, muse of poets,
the inspiration of artists forging elements to form,
speaking true words to open ears, riddles to closed hearts.

Listen, listen, listen to my sweetness,
my stillness is at the center of all things.
You who breathe and have a shape, come and drink of me.
Sing my praises, walk my land, forever bound to me.

Great goddess,
bless your women.
Bless the children.
Bless the wakening lands.
In the still soft voice is the one language that all may understand.

In Search of Crios Bríde

Barbara Callan

ignificant moments in our lives are sometimes planned, like the longed-for birth of a child. More often they are unexpected—the first meeting with a lover, the death of a parent, the dawning flash of insight, moments that come like the touch of a butterfly's wing. So it was for me that my first sight of the Crios Bríde ritual by a Renvyle hearth was an unexpected, heart-stopping moment, and in stepping through that circle of straw I began a journey to my spiritual homeland.

The year was 1990. The time was Brigit's Eve, the time to mark the passing from winter into spring, celebrated by the Celts as the festival of Imbolc at the beginning of February, and from early Christian times as Lá Fhéile Bríde or Saint Bridget's Day. It happened that my husband, Dave, was involved in a heritage project in the Letterfrack/Renvyle area of Connemara, led by archaeologist Erin Gibbons, and the group had decided to revive the custom of the *crios* Bríde, which had survived in the Renvyle area until well within living memory. I was lucky to be invited along to the re-enactment.

We set out on a night of some starlight and some rain, carrying the crios Bríde kindly provided by Paddy Fitzpatrick of Eagle's Nest and his mother Molly (a native Gaelic speaker, and as they say in these parts, "a mighty woman," who died in January 1997, aged 93). The *crios* turned out to be a *sugán* rope, or a rope plaiting from twisted strands of straw, joined to make a huge circle—big enough, as Paddy said, for a tall man to walk through. Indeed, one woman told us that her neighbor used to put her cows through it. "But she," she added, "was very religious!" Around the circumference were four small Brigit's crosses. Well instructed by

Paddy and Molly, our plan was to bring the *crios* from house to house as had always been done, though in this case we would especially target the houses where the old people lived.

At the first door we boldly knocked, our cry *"Ligig isteach Brighid agus a crios"* (Let in Brigit and her girdle!) hanging on the night air. Sure enough, the door was opened with the answer, *"Ceád mille fáilte romhat, a Bhrighid, is roimh do chrios!"* (A hundred thousand welcomes to Brigit and her girdle!"). In house after house we were welcomed in with a mixture of surprise, shock, wonder, and joy. Brigit was returning home.

The ritual involved each member of the household stepping through the *crios* three times clockwise, then gathering it up in their hands and passing it three times round their waists, while we chanted prayers in Irish all the while. Some of the old people had tears in their eyes. For us, there was an overwhelming surprise at the ritual's stunning power. To watch a family, from old grandmother to youngest child, go through the *crios* was moving beyond words. We were all spellbound, and before the night was out almost all of us would go through the *crios* ourselves.

Incoherent as I was about the experience, I remember on my way home coming to the awesome realization, "This is the goddess!" I was convinced that what I had taken part in was an ancient right of spring, a fertility rite. This intuition was confirmed for me five years later as I pored over Séamus Ó Catháin's *Festival of St. Brigit*, and found its first chapter brimful of lore on the fertility aspects of Brigit customs. In my understanding, fertility includes all aspects of creativity, but at that particular time literal fertility had a special relevance for me: nine months later, just before the festival of Samhain, I gave birth to a much-wanted second child.

I was later to learn that the *crios* Bríde custom was once widely practiced in Galway. As far as I am aware, in the manuscripts of the Irish Folklore Commission, there is no reference to the *crios* outside Galway and Mayo. However, in 1996 a Louth friend found a man in the Omeath district who knew how to make a different kind of *crios* and, intriguingly, it appears in Derry poet Seamus Heaney's poem "Crossings." So perhaps the use of the *crios* was more widespread than is recorded.

Soon after the event of the *crios* Bríde, I went to quiz my good friend Mary Coyne, who grew up on Inishbofin Island, off the Conne-mara coast. Had the *crios* Bríde been made on Inishbofin? No, it hadn't, but she remembered well the custom of the Brideóg (young Brigit) from her childhood. All the young girls from the village would go from house to house on Brigit's Eve carrying the Brideóg, a doll representing Brigit as a child. At each house they would be given some eggs, flour, sugar, or raisins. These offerings they brought back to one of their mothers, who would help them make cakes for a party held a few days later. Only the girls were allowed at this party, which of course led to attempted cake raids by the boys. The Brideóg was also the custom on Inishturk South, and indeed was widespread through the country—often, though not always, confined to girls. Overall, my feeling was and still is that these traditions of Brigit are of tremendous significance for women, a living link with a hidden spiritual heritage that celebrates the sacred feminine.

To the early Celts, Brigit was a triple goddess of poetry (and proph-ecy), healing, and smith-craft, as well as being concerned with childbirth and the abundance of crops. She was also, it would seem, strongly linked with the sun. In many ways, the lives and the folklore of Saint Bridget resonate with the symbols of the goddess. For example, Saint Bridget is associated with cows, and indeed with a white cow—the sacred white cow of the goddess— remembering Galway in the name Inishbofin or Inis Bó Finne (island of the white cow). The goddess Brigit is every-where connected with fire (fire of inspiration, fire of healing, and fire of transformation), and Saint Bridget's nuns at her convent in Kildare kept a sacred flame alight for many centuries. That fire was rekindled in 1993 by the Brigidine Sisters; perhaps part of what it stands for is a re-awakening of women.

In 1994, when I began to write songs, one of the first I wrote was "Amhrán Do Bhrighid," or "Song for Brigit," in which I tried to fuse together what Brigit had meant in the past and what she meant to me now. I was invited to bring this song to a women's gathering, Celebrating the Festival of Brigit, at the end of the following January in Termonfeckin, County Louth. Not too far from Termonfeckin is Faughart, reputed birthplace of Saint Bridget, which has several holy wells and a series of stones for healing different parts of the body. One of the wells is in a graveyard where, my father told me, many of my ancestors are buried. I readily agreed to come and offered to bring the *crios* Bríde.

I went to Paddy Fitzpatrick to ask if he would lend me the *crios* he had previously lent to the heritage group. He no longer had it. "But," he said, "I'll make you a new one, if we can get the straw." He needed oat straw for strength, he told me, and it had to be full sheaves, which meant it had to be hand-reaped. The problem was that very few people locally bothered growing oats any more, although formerly it was an integral part of farming practice. However, he would visit that evening the one man on the Renvyle Peninsula who might have it and, if he got it, he'd make the *crios* and bring it over to me in Cleggan.

Several days went by and no *crios*. I asked all over Cleggan for oat straw. Might there be some at Cleggan farms for the horses? Yes, there was indeed, but it turned out to be baled straw, chopped too small to be of any use. With only a few days to go, in desperation, I headed down to the pier to my friend Paddy Halloran, famous skipper of the Inishbofin ferry. By any chance would there by some oat straw on Inishbofin? "Oh, I doubt it very much," Paddy said slowly, "the old ways are gone on the island. But I'll certainly make inquiries for you." I could see Paddy warming to the challenge. An hour later, as I was collecting my son from the pierside playgroup, Paddy came running up, waving a piece of paper, "I have it for you! It's on Inishturk!"

The morning had seen the first break in weeks of bad weather and, of course, there was a boat in from Turk for supplies. Paddy had accosted young Augustine O'Toole, who said his father had some oat straw. My hopes rose—his father, Paddy O'Toole, is a friend and takes a great interest in folklore. I phoned him. Of course I could have some.

But what about the chance of another boat in, in the next few days? "Even if you can't get it to me in time, I'd still like to have it for the future, Paddy," I pleaded.

"Oh, don't worry, I'll do the best I can for you."

Next morning he phoned. "It's on the post-boat to Renvyle," he said. "I've asked him to deliver it to Paddy Fitz but I think it would be better if you could meet the boat."

I chased over to Renvyle by car.

The problem was to establish where the boat would come in. People had differing options—Gurteen pier, or back at Dooneen harbor—but luckily I spotted the Renvyle postman: he'd surely know. He directed me to a stony beach beyond Renvyle House. I ended up in Roz Coyne's house, overlooking the beach, chatting and drinking tea for an hour as we scanned the sea from Inishturk for signs of a post-boat. There were none. We mused about what the post-boat would look like—surely quite big. Just as I was phoning Dave in Letterfrack to see if he could wait any longer, a *currach** appeared from nowhere. But that couldn't be the post-boat, could it? "It could, it could," urged Dave.

And so it was that I went running down the beach at Renvyle, to meet a *currach* bearing the precious load of oat straw. As the boatman threw it across to me, I had the sense of plucking the last strands of a nearly forgotten tradition, from one of our western-most islands, to carry them back to the center. My running steps were in many senses a race against time. Almost without stopping, I sped back to the car, then it was up to Paddy Fitz's house, nestled under the mountain. His son, Johnny, met me.

"You got the straw."

"I did. Is Paddy in?"

"He is, but he's in bed with the flu."

"John, could you ever make it up for me?"

"Oh, don't worry, I'll get him up this evening and we'll do it together."

And they did. It was a most beautiful *crios* Bríde, of gleaming yellow straw interwoven with rushes "for the green of the spring," as Paddy explained. It turned out that he himself, on a visit to Turk, had helped to reap the straw. I brought the *crios* to Termonfecken, where it was the focus point of our opening ritual for women from all over Ireland. It stayed in our sacred space for the weekend for people to go through and, when we were leaving, it went to Northern Ireland, to some of the

---

* Editor's Note: A *currach* is a type of Irish boat with a wooden frame, over which animal skins or hides were once stretched, though now canvas is more usual.

women who help "turn back the streams of war," as was said of Saint Bridget herself. It seemed the right thing to do.

Later, Paddy agreed to make me another *crios*, this time with Dave as apprentice. This one, fittingly, was for a Brigit workshop in Letterfrack, where women from this area could explore some of the rich heritage kept alive in one of its last outposts, this corner of Connemara.

My story of the *crios* Bríde is one small link in the reappearance of Brigit as a source of inspiration in Ireland. This phenomenon has seemed to sweep the country in the last twenty years, touching people from all walks of life. One could say it signaled that it was time to develop a spirituality that is female-inclusive. And indeed, not all those re-attuned to Brigit have been women. In the folk tradition, the indications are that the Brideóg was originally a ritual involving young girls, and the *crios* Bríde was originally carried by young boys. Can we see our way to a spirituality that honors both the feminine and the masculine? That is one of the challenges for the new millennium.

Meanwhile, a beautiful *crios* Bríde, made from Inishturk oat straw by a group of women led by Mary Scanlan of Carraroe, found its way back to Inishturk for Lá Fhéile Bride 2000. And in the Renvyle peninsula, the *crios* Bríde tradition has spontaneously re-emerged.

REFERENCES:

Heaney, Seamus. 1993. *Seeing Things*. New York: Farrar, Strauss and Giroux.

Ó Cathain, Seamus. 1995. *The Festival of Brigid: Celtic Goddess and Holy Woman*. Ireland: DBA Publications.

Magdalen Rising: The Beginning

Elizabeth Cunningham

Magdalen Rising: The Beginning is the first of the four Maeve Chronicles, a series of novels featuring the feisty Celtic Magdalen, who is no one's disciple. In this excerpt, Maeve is at Druid school on the Isle of Mona. She has been concealing a pregnancy that is the result of rape. As the community on Mona celebrates Brigit's Day, she reveals her secret.

Soon it was lambing time, and the sense of crisis intensified. Birth after birth went wrong, with lots of ewes and lambs lost. The ewes who survived with living young had only the scantiest of milk. Then the feast of Imbolc (the name means ewe's milk) dawned cold and grey, confirmation that the cosmos was seriously out of whack. As a child on Tir na mBan, I had always loved this holiday. Imbolc marked the quickening of the year, the first secret stirrings of green life in the softening earth, the rekindling of the Bride's sacred flame. Since the formal version of my childhood name was Bride's Flame, I had always taken the holiday personally.

Now, despite my almost unassailable sense of well-being, I felt troubled. Imbolc, later celebrated as St. Brigid's day or Candlemas, was a particularly female holiday, bright with flame but also sweet and rich with new milk. Snow melted on mountain breasts and mammal breasts became fountains. Bride was the inspiration of poets and smiths. She was also midwife, wet nurse, and foster mother. Now that I felt so far removed in every sense from my mothers, I needed her to be my foster mother. As I looked around on that bleak, frozen morning, Bride was nowhere in sight.

Despite the bitter weather (why, I wondered once again, were the Crows and Cranes so inept at climate control?), the women who lived at Caer Leb gathered to begin the rites. Men would not be part of the ceremonies until later. We fashioned a Bride doll, dressed her in white, bedecked with shells and ribbons, then set her in a wicker cradle with an oak wand crowned with a shapely acorn, lying across her. Singing songs of praise, we processed with her from Caer Leb towards a spring that welled in the lap of an ancient oak, both the oak and the well being sacred to Bride. On the way, we were joined by women and girls from the farmsteads, and all their bony, female cattle. The maidens wore white (under their warmest cloaks) like the Bride doll. The women of childbearing age and older painted their faces with woad to honor the departing blue hag of winter—except that she wasn't departing, and the pinched faces of the young girls looked almost as blue as the woad-painted ones.

What should have been a joyous procession was all too somber as we shivered in the cold wind, bruising our feet on the frozen hummocks of winter fields that should have been ready for the first planting. The almost-dry ewes and their spindly lambs did not have the strength to bleat back and forth to each other as they usually did. There were no new greens in the fields to encourage them. Still, we sang as loudly and bravely as we could, praising our Bride, invoking her power and protection.

> Early on Bride's morn
> Shall the serpent come from the hole.
> I will not harm the serpent
> Nor will the serpent harm me.
> This is the day of Bride.
> The Queen shall come from the mound.

When we reached the spring, all but a small hole was covered with ice. We gathered round and breathed over the water, as if we had Bride's power to breathe life into the dead. Some of the ice melted. Between songs, women spoke to Bride and importuned her to bring them safely through childbirth. They made offerings of torques and brooches to the half-frozen well. As unobtrusively as I could, I removed the brooch pin from my cloak and tossed it into the cold, dark water. I had not thought much about the actual birth of my baby. It sounded as though I was going to need all the help I could get.

At sunset (such as it was, there being no light or color) the men arrived at the spring, headed up by the Cranes. They formed an outer circle around the women's inner circle. We had been singing and offering devotion to Bride all day. Now, with the Cranes present, the ceremony suddenly became official and formal. It irked me, this presumption that a rite could not seriously begin until the druids were there. I deliberately unleashed my attention and let it wander while the archdruid sang the quarters. I couldn't see much in the gloaming, but I thought I glimpsed the red of Foxface's beard across the circle from me. And could that be Esus standing next to him?

Then one of the Crows from Holy Isle came forward with a live ember from the sacred fire the Crows tended in a cave among their cliffs. This fire was never allowed to go out and was never extinguished, even on Samhain. With the coal, the ancient Crow (possibly the one who had shirked guard duty on Lughnasad) lit the bonfire that had been prepared next to the spring. Bride's flame leaped toward the heavy, starless sky. Above a mass of dark cloaks, faces appeared, suddenly bright, glowing in the light. I was right; Esus was standing next to Foxface. Their proximity made my stomach knot. The baby, sensing my disturbance, twisted restlessly. Then Esus caught my gaze and held it. The heat from the fire felt like a cool breeze in comparison to that one look passing between us.

In spite of my preoccupation, I began to pay attention again when the old archdruid stepped into the circle again and rooted himself there. He stood until it seemed as though he had grown there like the huge oak he so resembled. Like any ancient tree, he looked storm-rocked, scarred, bereft of a branch or two after the hard winter. But he was there, his being a testimony to endurance. In the presence of that potent stillness, the crowd calmed, more than calmed. We fell into a collective trance.

At a sign so subtle it must have been no more than the flickering of an eyebrow, the crowd shifted and made way. Flanked by two Crows, a white cow with red-brown ears stepped into the circle and approached the archdruid. Like all the cattle on Mona that winter, she was gaunt and her udder looked shriveled. Her horns had been decked with furze (the only live bloom to be found), dried heather bells, and rowan berries. Around her slack neck she wore a gold torque, specially fashioned for her, of twining snakes. No matter how much the winter had ravaged her, we knew whom she embodied.

A cry of greeting and beseeching rose from the crowd: Bride! Bride! Someone struck up a drum and we all began to sing to the docile (possibly sedated) cow as she came to stand before the druid, who greeted her ceremoniously. He bowed his head to her, then kissed her eyes and her nose. With a little help from the two Crows, he stooped and kissed her dry teats. Throughout his attentions, the cow remained calm, only flicking her tail now and again as if the archdruid were a pesky fly. When he straightened up, he came back to her head and began speaking to her in a low voice only she could hear. She appeared to pay grave attention, her head bent towards him, her tail perfectly still.

Gradually, the volume of the archdruid's voice rose so that we could all hear him addressing Bride, with consistent poetic meter, in formal Q-Celtic. He told her of the hard winter and the hard ground, the hard births and the hard, ungiving teats of the ewes and the cows. (As if she didn't know, being a cow herself at the moment.) At last he beseeched her for a sign. Tell us what is wrong, he begged her. What must the Combrogos do?

The old cow listened ruminatively—cows are ruminators, after all—moving her jaws in the same rhythm as the druid's speech. When he had done, she continued to chew thoughtfully for a time, apparently unmoved by all the expectation focused on her. Then slowly, serenely, she lifted her head, looking around the circle—until she locked eyes with me.

You must have looked into a cow's eyes before. You know how mild that gaze is, how benign and bemused. Bride, in her form as a white cow with red ears, looked at me that way, without urgency but steadily, leaving me in no doubt that she had a message, and the message was for me.

Despite Bride's reputation as a poet, she did not speak in words. She sent images to my mind. I saw the bleak, grey cloud that had covered Mona all winter, the high, unyielding cloud that doesn't temper the cold but seals it in. Then I saw beyond the cloud cover to the clear, shining, near-full moon. That image dissolved, and I saw myself from the outside, as if I were someone else. I saw myself cloaked and concealed in my heavy, grey cloak. Just as I had seen beyond the clouds before, I saw through my garments to the round, glowing moon underneath. All the while these images came and went, I saw her eyes—the cow's, Bride's. The reflection of flame flickered in their depth.

I don't know how to describe what happened next, except to say that Bride communicated her whole nature to me: the divine and the bovine. I was myself, Maeve, fifteen-year-old girl, six months pregnant, and I was also the goddess. We had been singing to Bride and calling her all day. Now she was here, if I would let her be. That's what she asked of me, the mild-eyed, starving cow. I stepped into the circle. The cow, already looking in my direction, turned fully toward me. Just as on the day of the caber toss, my awareness narrowed and intensified. I could not hear the murmuring of the crowd or the sharp admonishments of Crows or Cranes. All human emotion was a flickering of energy on the periphery, like silent heat lightning. I undid the knot of thorn that had fastened my cloak since I'd tossed my brooch into the spring. A droplet of blood appeared on my thumb, but I felt no pain. Then I reached for the hem of my tunic and pulled it over my head. It joined the cloak on the ground, a layer of green over the grey.

The holy cow gave a long, low moo, tossed her garlanded head and retreated into the crowd. The archdruid and the Crows backed away from me, perhaps inadvertently. There I stood, in the center of the circle, naked. All around me, there was what you might call a willing suspension of disbelief. Yes, think of me as a suspension bridge, spanning a great chasm, holding the tension of the moment in balance. Or think of me as one glistening thread of the web, suddenly illuminated, making the pattern visible for an instant. No one spoke, no one made a move to stop me. For an instant, I could do whatever I wanted—or rather whatever was wanted in that moment, by that moment.

I just stood for a time with the firelight playing over my body. I gazed at my breasts. They were fuller than ever, their blue veins matching the blue at the base of the flames. The nipples had the almost golden cast of bare mountain tops at sunrise. Round as my breasts were, my belly now was rounder. I could see its full-moon curve rising over their peaks. With the cold of winter and the necessity for concealment, I'd scarcely had a chance to simply marvel at myself. Now I did. Never mind that I was standing in the midst of several hundred people. Slowly I turned in a circle, looking at my belly in all lights and angles. As I turned, a fresh wind began to blow—a soft, warm wind. It smelled of wet earth. It bore the scent of blossom and fruit from the magical orchard of Tir na mBan. I recognized, too, the spicy smell of the Temple gardens where I had been a dove in Anna's hand.

Gently, the wind pushed the clouds aside. Overhead, the almost full moon echoed the curve of my belly. The Combrogos began to weep.

At the sound, my breasts tingled and burned the way my hands do when the fire of the stars pours through them, and my nipples began to spray a fountain of golden milk. Then, you might say, all heaven broke loose. The cows lowed and sheep bleated loudly. A cry went up from the crowd.

"The ewes are in milk! The ewes are in milk!" And then someone shouted: "The snakes are awake. The snakes are awake!"

From the rocks around the spring, two snakes emerged, coiling and uncoiling, and began gliding in my direction. When they reached my feet and began to twine themselves round my ankles, the crowd went crazy.

"Bride! Bride herself!"

They began to surge towards me, a huge wave of human passion that threatened to take me under or sweep me out to sea, far, far beyond my depth. It is dangerous to be adored. It can be fatal. The Cranes and the Crows acted quickly and no doubt saved my life. Linking arms, they surrounded me, a black and white barrier reef, and stood fast till the ecstasy began to ebb.

"My Combrogos!" said the archdruid, holding out his staff, then rooting it again. "As Bride is the goddess of the hearth's flame, go home now and celebrate her with laughter and song, with cakes and ale. Then rise up early tomorrow to sow the first seeds in the ready ground. Let the earth quicken. That is what Bride desires of you. That is why she appeared to you in this guise. To your hearths now, all."

When the last of the crowd had wafted away, like the last wisp of cloud or smoke, the Cranes and the Crows, who had been facing outward, dropped their arms as one and turned in on me. Then they linked arms again.

I was caught.

FORGING

Eileen Rosensteel

In her workshop,
on an icy February morning,
Brigit lights the fire.
Feeding it, with fuel and breath,
watching colors shift in the flames,
building heat.
She wraps her stiff leather apron around
as she chooses the metal
to go deep into the fire.
Pulling it out, glowing white,
on the anvil she strikes,
metal begins to sing.
The hammer falls over and over,
clang, clang, clang, thud
time to reheat,
back into the fire to soften,
stretching and shaping,
burning away impurities.
Her muscles work,
sweat drips down her back,
falls between her breasts,
damp hair escapes her braid,
as she pounds.

Folding metal upon itself,
with heat, muscle, rhythm,
forming a blade
following its song.
The poetry of metal,
a sharp edged tool.

THE SEARCH FOR BRIDE'S WELL

Cheryl Straffon

rigit was one of the principal Celtic goddesses, celebrated throughout the pagan Celtic world as the goddess of healing, smith-craft, and poetry. She is particularly associated with wells and her main festival was that of Imbolc, which celebrated her return to the land, seen in the lactation of the ewes and the first flowers of spring. She was so important a goddess that the Christian Church could not suppress her. Instead they turned her into Saint Bridget, and she became one of the most revered saints of the early Celtic Church. Legends and customs associated with her can be found in most Celtic lands, in particular in Scotland (where Bride's Well can be found on the Isle of Lewis) and in Ireland, where she is still venerated until this day.

Although there are many legends and stories about her in Ireland, and to a lesser extent in Scotland, it has always puzzled me that she appeared to have no particular place in the folklore and mythology of Cornwall, which was originally a P-Celtic (Brythonic) country, with a

language and culture similar to that of Wales and Brittany. However, if one looks beneath the surface, some traces of her can be found and, in particular, one holy well is named after her.

From the 5th to the 7th century CE, there were definite links between

Cornwall, then part of the kingdom of Dumnonia, and other Celtic lands, principally Ireland and Wales. It appears that early potters came from Ireland to Wales and then on to Cornwall, probably landing in the Tintagel area and settling initially along the valley of the River Camel, as Charles Thomas argues. There are the well-known labyrinth carvings on the walls of Rocky Valley near Tintagel, which are undated but could easily be from this period. There is also a little-known link between them and Ireland, for on a rock found at Hollywood near Glendalough in County Wicklow, and now in a museum in Dublin, another labyrinth carving offers an exact mirror image of the Rocky Valley ones—Rocky Valley being a left-handed and Wicklow Hills a right-handed labyrinth carving, according to Nigel Pennick. I would suggest that both carvings may have been made by the same peoples, who left their mark in their homeland of Ireland, and travelled to Cornwall, where they carved its mirror image as a thanksgiving for their safe arrival.

There are other clues to the links between Ireland and Cornwall from this time: many of the early saints were supposed to have come from Ireland and Wales, and several of the names are common to the three countries and nowhere else. For example, Saint Breaca, who gave her name to Breage in Cornwall, was supposed to have been born in East Meath in Ireland and educated at Saint Bridget's convent nearby. So if the Celts did travel trade routes here, they must have brought their legends and beliefs with them. One of the principal beliefs would have been of the pagan Bride, given a thin veneer of Christian nomenclature as Saint Bridget. There was a shrine to her at Kildare in Ireland tended by nineteen priestesses (later nuns), and Saint Bride's Bay on the coast of Wales, where the Irish migrants would have landed, was named after her. As they moved across Cornwall on the old route through Launceston and on into Devon, it seems to me unlikely that they would not have left some mark behind of her central presence in their lives.

For me, the breakthrough came when I started work on my book, *Pagan Cornwall: Land of the Goddess*, and subsequently, *The Earth Goddess*. I had been working on the hypothesis that the Cornish legend of Tristan and Iseult, first written down in the Medieval period, rep-

resented, in the character of Iseult, a localized version of the Goddess
Brigit. I had been searching for places in Cornwall connected to Iseult
and, in the course of that, began searching for holy wells that might have
been linked to the story. While researching the possible Irish trade routes
across North Cornwall, I found a reference in North Cornwall to a well
dedicated to Saint Bridget at map reference SX3500 7962. Here was the
missing link I had been seeking!

However, there appeared to be no source material on this well at all.
No books listed it—not even Meyrick's comprehensive collection of over
130 Cornish wells—and there was no information on it in the Sites and
Monuments Register of what was then the Cornwall Archaeological Unit.
The name was the clue I had been seeking but, for all I knew, the well
itself may have been a muddy hole in the ground or simply a lost
tradition.

So, in 1993, on a beautiful early spring day in February, Brigit's
month, I travelled with a friend through the snowdrop-filled lanes of
North Cornwall to the spot given on the map, and discovered we were
entering the private estate of Landue, near Lezant. *Lezant* is Cornish for
"holy place," and *landue* probably means "sanctuary," so our surmise
was that we had stumbled upon the site of a very early holy well around
which a sacred settlement had grown. Confirmation for this came later
in the discovery that a chapel to Saint Bridget was also recorded there.
On our way, we had stopped at the cross of Holyway (SX 2727 8232),
another clue to the route followed by the early migrants. Traced further
eastwards, one comes to Bridestow in Devon (literally, Bride's Place).
So it seems we had found the early route from the Rocky Valley through
the Camel Valley, Landue, and on to Devon. Perhaps the Irish and Welsh
Celtic migrants were only following a well-known trade route of their
ancestors from the sacred lands of Ireland to the sacred sites of Dartmoor.

But what of Bridget's Well? A special delight awaited us. By the
kind permission of the owner of the estate, we followed a secret path
through a bower of trees surrounded by snowdrops and early daffodils to
a beautiful well. The old gate was kept in place with shining white quartz
stones, and when we gently removed them and opened the gate, the water

was clear and fresh. The mid-day sun shone through the trees straight into the well, with all the stones glistening deep red and brown. It was an enchanted place!

We thanked Brigit for bringing us there and showing us the well, a well hidden for so many years, yet quietly cared for and looked after. Talking to the owner a little later, she told us that, in fact, a number of other wells in the area were also called by the local people Bridget's Well. There are no others listed on the map or in the SMR, so this is likely to be a very old folk memory of the importance of the area as a settlement on the trail, a trail I was now beginning to call Bride's Way.

And so the search was completed. It had taken me a full year to track down and discover the presence of Brigit in Cornwall, and the route taken by the Celtic forbears who brought her here from Ireland. There is further research to be done on other possible significant places along the way, and the links between the Insular Celts and their Continental cousins. But for the moment I was content to have discovered the gift of Bride in Cornwall, and her special place in my life and my researches.

REFERENCES:

Meyrick, J. 1982. *A Pilgrims Guide to the Holy Wells of Cornwall*. Falmouth: Meyrick.

Pennick, Nigel, 1992. *Mazes and Labyrinths*. London: Robert Hale.

Thomas, Charles. 1994. *And Shall These Mute Stones Speak?* Cardiff: University of Wales Press.

Straffon, Cheryl. (1994) 2012. *Pagan Cornwall—Land of the Goddess*. St. Just: Meyn Mamvro Publications.

—*1997. The Earth Goddess. London: Cassell*

Forging Finer Metal

Barbara Ardinger

Bright Blessed Lady, source of the craftsman's fire—
shoot your holy flame into my hands
into my heart
into my eyes and ears.
Bless me with your light.
I want to work in your forge,
I want to dance and sing for you,
and so I pray to you.
I want to forge finer metal to shine like you.
I want to bear my opening heart into a world that must be healed,
a world whose light, like yours, has been put out.
I want to find the flames of your wisdom
in myself.
Bright Blessed Lady, assign me to work in your forge
so that every bit of gold and good in me
rises up
to the magic.
Make me taller, stronger, keener,
make me a finer metal
so that I can defend you from those who would put out your light
again.

BRIGHDE OF THE ISLES

*Jill Smith**

Although born in England, I knew I had come home the first time I stepped onto the shores of the Western Isles of Scotland, also known as the Outer Hebrides. A few years later, I moved here and lived for ten years with my youngest son in an old house with no electricity and only cold water. I moved to Glastonbury for another decade while my son completed his education but, dearly as I love that place, living there only proved to me beyond any doubt that my true, deep, and only heart, spiritual, and physical home could be nowhere but the Western Isles. In 2008, I returned.

These islands sit in the Atlantic 23 miles west of the top northwest part of the Highlands of Scotland. Nowadays they are one of the strongest outposts of the Free Presbyterian Church, but there is something profoundly magical and mystical about them that blends in with the reality of everyday life. One thing I like about living here is that the people and the lives they lead are "real" in a way that many people's lives have ceased to be, especially some of those living in cities.

People call these islands "remote," but remote from what? Anciently, they sat on an oceanic super-highway for shipping. Even in very ancient times, boats travelled from Scandinavia, across the top of Scotland, and then down past the Hebrides to Ireland. The stretch of water between the mainland and the Hebrides, called the Minch, is very stormy and often

---

* Editor's Note: This article is largely extracted from Jill Smith's book *Mother of the Isles*, published in 2003 by Dor Dama Press, now available from www.jill-smith.co.uk.

more difficult to navigate than the Atlantic seas to the west; so there was a greater cultural connection between the people of the islands (the Gaelic-speaking Celts of Ireland) and the Nordic peoples (who, indeed, invaded and owned the islands for a long time) than there was to the Scottish mainland.

These islands are very powerful. Living here, this is something I sometimes forget—until I am with people visiting them for the first time and I see how profoundly they are affected by encountering the place. This is what happened to me when I first came here.

I was initially pulled here by the famed Callanish Stones and by a beautiful mountain in the form of a sleeping woman who gives birth to a new lunar cycle every nineteen years. But once here I felt a life force in the land, which was unlike anything I'd experienced anywhere before. It seemed to have an identity and, gradually, I began to realize this was—and is—Brighde, as her name is spelled here. She is the living spirit of place. She is the energy of the islands. She and the islands are manifestations of each other. So I came to know her, love her, and, in a way, depend on her. She was a strength that seemed to be with me, not only here, but wherever I went; an energy that pulled me back when I was away too long.

There are many manifestations of Brigit, just as there are many forms of her name, but here she has a very particular identity as Brighde of the Isles. She was anciently a goddess but, with the coming of Christianity, such was her hold on the hearts of the people that she was easily assimilated. She retained her own unique identity as Brighde of the Isles—part goddess, part saint, and yet something beyond either. She became part of people's everyday lives, particularly women's. They called on her with prayers and incantations, asking her help and blessing, not only for the major life events of childbirth, but for the daily tasks such as the *smooring* (covering) of the fire to keep it alight throughout the night.

She was so dear to the people that she even retained her female identity when becoming a saint, whereas some goddesses became male. Neither was she eclipsed by Mary, mother of Christ, though she was often known as "Mary of the Gaels." Sometimes, the Gaelic Saint Bride took on a Christian role that brought biblical events and characters into a

Hebridean setting; at other times she was transported geographically and even temporally to take part in events in Biblical lands.

Many have suggested that the word *hebrides* means "Brighde's islands," though this is uncertain. It has also been said that her name came from roots that mean "the exalted one" or "divinity," so her name may simply mean "goddess." Others believe it comes from the word "bright," indicating a manifestation of spiritual fire, the flame of Imbolc or Candlemas. She is thus also associated with the fire of poetic inspiration.

Many years ago, I was fascinated and inspired by the writings of Mary Beith, who wrote of traditional herbal and healing methods. She suggested that Brighde was linked to a long line of ancient mother goddesses associated with the moon, water, serpents, and weaving. She linked Brighde with the Libyan snake goddess, Neit, who protected women, childbirth, and marriage, and was skilled in the domestic arts. Brighde is credited with bringing many arts and crafts to humans, especially women, including spinning, weaving, and the tending of cattle. She is said to have brought the knowledge of tweed weaving to the women of Harris, as well as the sophisticated craft of dying the colors of the threads.

Beith suggested the snake's movement is like the complex weaving movements of the moon across the sky—the monthly, yearly, and nineteen-year cycles. Through this weaving of threads, complex lunar-astronomical knowledge was passed down through generations. Songs accompanied the weaving, some to help memorize the order of the colors of threads; maybe it was in this way that more esoteric knowledge was also passed on. Threads were important in the Gaelic healing rituals of the Highlands and Islands. The *eolas an t-snaithen* (charms of the threads) involved the use of red, white, and black threads to represent the eclipsed moon, the full moon, and the dark moon.

In Gaelic Christian tradition, Brighde was said to have been a maidservant at an inn in the time of drought. She was left alone with only enough food and water for herself for a day. When Mary and Joseph called, Brighde gave Mary the water and bread. Back indoors, she found there was as much as there had been before. Later, she saw light round the barn and rushed over to become the aid-woman at the birth of Christ, so becoming known as *ban-chuideachaidh Moire* (the aid-woman of Mary) and later *muime chriosda* (foster-mother of Christ), fostering being common in Celtic traditions. Women of the Highlands and Islands gave birth on one knee, which is why midwives were often known as "knee-women," and Brighde was the knee-woman of Mary. She was therefore invoked to aid and protect at times of birth.

The mother of Brighde was said to have given birth to her while carrying a pitcher of milk, and in this she gave the babe her first bath. Brighde was also said to have been born as her mother stood on the threshold of a house, so she was of both mortal and otherworldly realms. Brighde was then said to have been raised on the milk of a   white red-eared cow—a faerie cow and the color of the full moon.

In one story connected to the Callanish stones, a woman went to the shore in a time of famine to drown herself so her husband and children could have their little remaining food. But a beautiful white cow with red ears appeared and spoke to her in Gaelic. She told the woman to fetch her milk pail and tell her neighbors to do the same and to gather at the Callanish stones. They did so and every woman was able to fill her pail. They did the same each evening throughout the winter and thus survived the famine. This went on as long as each woman only brought one pail, but one night a "wicked witch" came with two pails. The cow would have none of it and refused her any milk. The witch returned the next night with only one pail, but she had replaced the bottom with a sieve and milked the cow dry. The cow was never seen at the stones again. I feel surely this cow was a manifestation of Brighde providing for her people through a time of crisis, and teaching to take only what you need.

In another story, a fairy inhabited a tree on a knoll. She summoned women to gather there on a certain day and promised she would give them the "milk of wisdom." Many did as the fairy asked, and she appeared holding the *copan Moire* (cup of Mary), which was the "blue-eyed" limpet shell containing the milk of wisdom. She invited each woman to drink until there was none left. Any woman who arrived late would find there was "no wisdom left for them." In *Scottish Folklore*, Mackenzie says he believes this story is the memory of a milk goddess; I believe that goddess to be Brighde.

So Brighde became connected to Imbolc, when ewes give birth and come into milk. She is also connected with "milk-yielding" plants, which are sacred to her. The dandelion in Gaelic is *bearnan Bride* (little notched plant of Brighde) and its milk-like sap is food for early lambs. Brighde was invoked when plucking the *torranan* (figwort), a rare plant that grows in rocky places and bears a white flower resembling a woman's breast. The flower fills with dew when the tide is rising and dries up with the ebbing, so it must be picked on the incoming tide. The flower would be placed under the milk pail, the woman having first carried it three times *deosil* (sun-wise) around the pail while the invocation was recited. Soon the pail would be overflowing with creamy, rich, sweet milk.

In the Hebrides, Brighde was also known as *Brighde nam brat* (Bride of the mantle), from the story in which Saint Bride was travelling to take her vows as a nun. She had to cross a dangerous bog but, as she stepped onto it, it turned into a green meadow full of spring flowers. The goddess/saint thus spread her mantle of spring over the land.

Brighde's breath was said to give new life to the dead, breathing the new life of the growing year into the mouth of the dead of winter. It was said, "Winter [would] open its eyes to the tears and smiles, the sighs and the laughter of spring" and "the venom of the cold" would tremble for its safety on Brighde's Day. She was also known as *Brighde binn nam bas ban* (melodious Brighde of the fair palms). It was said that, on her day, she would put her palm in water and the "venom" or the sting of winter's cold would be gone.

As both goddess and saint, Brighde presided over poetry and smithcraft as well as healing. As a fire goddess, she held, and gave, the "fiery arrow" of poetic inspiration, and also the transformative fire of the hearth and the smith's forge. The Christian festival of Candlemas seems to have come initially from pagan Roman celebrations of Februa, the mother of Mars. The Church couldn't suppress the lighting and processing of candles at that time, so found its own stories to accompany these activities. Forty days after giving birth, Jewish mothers went to the temple to present the child and to be purified after the birth. It was said that, on Mary's way to the temple, Brighde walked before her carrying a lighted candle in each hand. Even though there was a strong wind blowing, these candles never flickered, so this day became *Latha Feille Brighde* (Day of the Festival of Brighde).

Two birds are dedicated to Brighde: the linnet, *bigein Brighde* (little bird of Brighde), who whistles a welcome to her; and the oyster-catcher, which is the *ghillie-Brighde* (Bride's servant). The red, white, and black of the oyster-catcher originally symbolized the eclipsed, full, and dark moon colors of the lunar goddess Brighde. Christian stories connected with these birds evolved as Brighde became a saint, telling how the welfare of her foster son, Christ, was her great concern. In one story, he was chased by his enemies and came exhausted to a shore. Two oyster-catchers laid him between rocks and covered him with seaweed. When his enemies arrived, the birds flew up, making a great noise as though no one had been there before to disturb them. Christ's enemies thought he could not have passed that way, and they left. Since then, the oyster-catcher has shown a white cross on a black ground when it flies.

As in many places where belief in Brighde was strong, there was a place called Kilbride (Church of Bride) on South Uist. Legend has it that Brighde came ashore here when she visited the Outer Isles, and when she did so she had an oyster-catcher standing on each wrist, like a pair of hawks. One writer has said that, in the first half of the 18th century, the whole of Harris was known as Kilbride.

The traditions of Brighde continued later in the southern parts of the Outer Isles, which are Catholic, and in parts of the Highlands. Until comparatively recently, Brighde's day was greatly celebrated in those parts. In the Highlands, young girls made a figure of Brighde from a sheaf of corn, usually oats. They dressed her and decorated her with sparkly shells and crystals, and any small flowers and greenery growing at that time of year, and placed a very bright shell or crystal over her heart. This was called *reul iuil Brighde* (guiding star of Brighde). The girls, dressed in white and with their hair loose, carried Brighde in a procession, singing her a song and visiting every house, where she was offered more shells and flowers. Mothers gave her a Brighde *bannock* (bread), cheese, or roll of butter. Finally, they went to one house to make a feast, with men being allowed in later. Much food was kept by and later distributed to the poor.

In another tradition, the older women of each household made a cradle called the bed of Brighde. They shaped a figure of her from a sheaf of oats and decorated her with ribbons, shells, and crystals. One woman would go to the door and stand on the threshold, put her hands on the door jambs and call softly in Gaelic, "Brighde's bed is ready." Another woman would say, "Brighde come in, thy welcome is truly made." They would then ask for a blessing on the house, and Brighde's spirit would enter the Brighde figure. The women would place the figure in the bed with a straight, white wand beside her (the *slachdan Brighde*), usually made of birch, broom, bramble, white willow, or other sacred wood stripped of its bark. The women then smoothed over the ashes of the hearth, which was in the center of the floor. In the morning, they eagerly examined the ashes, being very pleased if they found the mark of her wand, but overjoyed if they found her footprint. They knew then that she had truly been with them that night and that they would have good fortune and plenty throughout the coming year. They often left something on the door jamb, on the door, or in the doorway, so that as Brighde entered she would touch it. They would carry or wear this for the rest of the year as blessing or protection.

One Imbolc, early in the years of my life on Lewis, I enacted this ritual with my young son, who was then about three years old. It was one of the most powerful experiences of my life, and I do believe Brighde entered our house and gave us her blessing.

A special verse was recited on Brighde's morn:

Early on Brighde's morn
The serpent shall come from the hole.
I will not harm the serpent
Nor will the serpent harm me.

Here, either the goddess of spring or the serpent life force of the earth awakened and emerged after the death of winter. It is interesting to recall that the serpent's movements also represented the weaving of the moon across the heavens.

In the Hebrides, line fishermen cast lots for fishing banks on Brighde's day; the raven built its nest, the skylarks began to sing, and the coming of Brighde inspired hope in people's hearts after the long, dark winter.

There are many beautiful incantations and prayers in the *Carmina Gadelica*, Carmichael's great collection of Scottish traditional poems, which invoke Brighde's blessing both for the ordinary tasks of the day and the greater events of life. For example, when covering the fire with ash to keep it through the night, a prayer was spoken to "Brighde of the kindly fires." She was often referred to as "beloved Brighde," and was very dear to the hearts of the people.

Although the northern Outer Isles are now Presbyterian, there are still ancient, ruined chapels with dedications to the saints. At Melbost Borve on the northwest of Lewis, one chapel in a very ruinous state is dedicated to Brighde—a small, oval shape with the remains of an ancient graveyard nearby. Not far away, a beautiful well, Tobar Brighde, is also dedicated to her. When I first knew it, a fence with a little gate surrounded it, but this gradually fell down and hasn't been replaced, so the well now lies in open croftland. The water is clear and clean, though these days the stream gets clogged up with mats of grass growing over it. Anyone visiting should clear it so the water can flow away from the well, which must be fed by a spring.

I used to feel there must be some old ladies who tended it. I once had a conversation with an elderly lady, not long before she died, who lived nearby and seemed to love the well dearly. She confirmed that she and another lady used to keep it clean, filling it with stones so the water level would drop when the stones were removed and then they could scour the sides with heather. She told me it never ran dry, and even in times of drought people would come from miles around to sit for an hour while their pail filled.

On the capstone of the well, there is a thin layer of cement in which the imprint of a horseshoe has been made. The lady said a relative of hers put it there "for luck" but, whether knowingly or not, it seems to honor and acknowledge Brighde of smith-craft. It is a beautiful spot, a wonderful place to sit at Imbolc and watch the sun set over the sea and the waves crash on the rocks and rattle the stones on the shore. The nearby shore is called Eire. At sunrise, there used to be many oyster-catchers on the next croft, though I've not seen them there for a few years. When there is a full moon at Imbolc, this place is like another realm; when there is a crescent moon, it is like the horseshoe forged by Brighde. Sometimes, if you are very lucky, you may even see the magical curtains of the Aurora Borealis wafting in the northern skies, bringing one very close to the otherworld. Brighde is very close at that spot; she and the power of her land fill the heart even more than usual at this, her very special time of year.

REFERENCES:

Beith, Mary. 1992. *The Healing Threads*. Edinburgh: Polygon.

Carmichael, Alexander. 1992. *Carmina Gadelica*. Edinburgh: Floris.

Mackenzie, Donald A. 1935. *Scottish Folklore and Folklife Studies*. Glasgow: Blackie.

Swire, Otto F. 1966. *The Outer Hebrides and their Legends*. Edinburgh: Oliver and Boyd.

Goddess of Smiths

Mael Brigde

breath dissolving iron
liquid bronze and gold
white heat who destroys
with one cruel blow
you guide the hammer   Brigit
death and life together
forging to shatter
shattering to forge anew

and what is fashioned
cookpot for the hospitaller
vast enough to hold a cow
ale crock   chariot furnishing
offering dish   cloak pin
sword

beat me on your anvil   Brigit
melt me in your pot
knit me solid
make me whole
bring from me a fine-bossed cauldron
offering to your endless round

in this life and the next
this life and the next

Bride in Scotland

Stuart McHardy

The Scottis, Peychtes, Britanis, Inglismen & Irishmen with sik
veneratione in ilk place have honoured S Brigida, that innumer-
able kirkes erected to God, amang them ale, to her, ye sal se; yie
and mae to her than to ony of the rest: the Irland men contendes
that her haly body thay have with thame in that toune quhilke
thay cal Dun, in quhilke place the body of thair Apostle S. Patrik
is keipet. our cuntrey men ascrynes the same Glore unto thame,
quha thinkes, that hitherto thay have honouret it in the Chanrie
of Abernethie, & richtlie have done thay think.

The Scots, Picts and Britons, Englishmen and Irishmen with
such veneration in each place have honored Saint Brigit, that
innumerable churches erected to God, amongst them all, to her,
ye shall see; yes and more to her than to any of the rest; the Irish
men contend that her holy body they have with them in that town
which they call Dun, in which place the body of their apostle
St Patrick is kept. Our countrymen ascribe the same Glory unto
themselves, who think, that hitherto they have honoured it in the
Canonry of Abernethy, and rightly have done, they think.

his paragraph from Jhone Leslie's 16th century *Historie of Scotland* clearly shows that contemporary Scots thought of Saint Bridget as an essentially indigenous figure, and not an import from Ireland. While it seems clear that there are grounds for understanding the original Christian Saint Bridget as being Irish, the figure behind her—Bride—is, as Leslie suggests, rooted in Scottish culture. However, the concentration by scholars on early Irish source materials has led to a situation where the Scottish material has been neglected. This is unfortunate because, as we shall see, Bride in Scottish tradition is a figure of substantial interest.

Scottish history and folklore have been long bedeviled by the idea that the Scots themselves came from Ireland to Argyll in the 6th century. This idea, which appears most likely to have been a Christian construct, has been shown as erroneous by Ewan Campbell in his seminal article, "Were The Scots Irish?" As he shows, there is no contemporary historical support, and no actual archaeological or linguistic evidence, to support the idea, which first crops up in Bede's decidedly non-contemporaneous *History of the English Church and People*. In *The Pagan Symbols of the Picts*, I have suggested that the very idea of this Irish intrusion may have been Christian propaganda, perhaps to diminish the importance of the pre-Christian sacred landscape of Kilmartin in Argyll, and there is no doubt that the Irish connection was seen as of major importance by the post-7th century Christian Church in Britain. They placed great emphasis on the role of the Irish Saint Columba, who became the patron saint of Scotland; his influence—and thus Irish influence—on Scottish history and culture has long been presented as of primary importance.

However, the evidence we have shows Bride to be as indigenous to Scotland as to Ireland and, given the likelihood of some kind of link between Bride and the Brigante tribe of northern England, as noted by Anne Ross in *Pagan Celtic Britain*, it would appear that she was a widespread figure in the culture of the pre-Christian tribal societies of both Ireland and the northern areas of the British Isles.

Marian McNeill, in *The Silver Bough*, pointed out that, in Scotland, Bride is associated in several prayers and incantations with the serpent. In Scottish terms, this must mean the adder, Scotland's only indigenous snake, and it is surely relevant that the adder crops up so widely on Pictish symbol stones. McNeill gives this version of a hymn to the adder emerging from its hibernation on Imbolc, Saint Bride's Day:

Today is the day of Bride
the serpent shall come from the hole
I will not molest the serpent
Nor will the serpent molest me.

McNeill also makes mention of an actual rite of the serpent taking place in Skye and, while these activities have, in the past, been regarded as a relic of serpent worship, it is perhaps more accurate to say that the serpent/adder is a symbol associated with the concept of a goddess figure. It is particularly apt as a symbol of fertility, more specifically regeneration, as it seems to disappear into the earth through the winter, like seeds that are planted in autumn, lie dormant, and come up in the spring. The annual replacement of serpent's skin is also symbolic of rebirth and regeneration.

In this respect, we should perhaps remember that there are no snakes in Ireland. The famous story of Saint Patrick having driven all the serpents from Ireland has long been interpreted as having overcome the pre-Christian priesthood, often referred to as Druids, who were symbolized by the adder. However, the biological reality is that there is no evidence of snakes existing in Ireland at any point since the last Ice Age, and thus the association of the "serpent" with Bride emphasizes her indigenousness in Scotland.

McNeill tells us of other rites associated with Bride. It seems that, in many parts of the Highlands, on the eve of Bride's Day, groups of women would gather together and make an oblong basket they called *leaba* Bride, the bed of Bride, which they would decorate. Then, taking a selected sheaf of corn, they would fashion it into the shape of a woman and " . . . deck this ikon with gay ribbons from the loom, sparkling shells from the sea, and bright stones from the hill." Afterwards, when it was dressed and decorated, one woman would go to the door of the house and, standing on the step with her hands on the jambs, call softly into the darkness, "Bride's bed is ready." To this, a ready woman behind would reply, "Let Bride come in. Bride is welcome." The woman at the door would again address Bride: "Bride come thou in, thy bed is made. Preserve the house for the Trinity."

The women would then place the icon of Bride with great ceremony in the bed. They would place a small, straight, white wand (the bark being peeled off) beside the figure. The wand was generally of birch, broom, bramble, white willow, or other sacred wood, with *crossed* (banned) wood being carefully avoided. The women would then level the ashes on the hearth, smoothing them carefully. In the early morning, the family would closely scan the ashes. If they found the mark of the wand of Bride, they would rejoice, but if they found *lorg Bride* (the footprint of Bride), their joy was very great: this was a sign that Bride was present with them during the night, and was favorable to them, and that there would be an increase in family, flock, and field in the coming year. Should there be no marks on the ashes, the family would be dejected. They would consider it a sign that she was offended and would not hear their call. To propitiate her and gain her ear, the family would offer oblations and burn incense on the hearth.

McNeill is here referencing Carmichael's *Carmina Gadelica*, which was published at the beginning of the 20th century, and it is notable that these practices were recorded as happening in communities that had been ostensibly Christian for considerably more than a thousand years. This underlines the hold that the idea of Bride, an aspect of the mother goddess, continued to have on both community and individuals until relatively recently.

Two important motifs concerning Bride are her portrayal as the goddess of summer, and the tale of the *cailleach* changing into Bride after drinking from a sacred well on Imbolc, the day dedicated to Bride and Saint Bridget. This is how Marian NcNeill gives the first story in *The Silver Bough*:

> Bride is kept prisoner all winter in Ben Nevis, where she awaits
> her rescuer, Aengus of the White Steed, Aengus the Ever-Young,
> who has his home in that green island of perpetual summer that

drifts about on the silver tide of the Atlantic. Aengus beholds Bride in a dream, and sets out to succour her, riding on his milk-white steed with flowing mane over the Isles and over the Minch. The Cailleach strives in vain to keep them apart, and the Day of Bride Celebrates their union.

The second motif links the figure of Bride directly to that of the *cailleach*, the hag of winter whose attributes of weather-working and landscape formation clearly mark her out as having been, at one time, a mother goddess figure. McNeill informs us:

> On the eve of Bride, the Cailleach repairs to the Isle of Youth, in whose woods lies the miraculous Well of Youth. There, at the first glimmer of dawn, before any bird has sung or any dog barked, she drinks of the water that bubbles in a crevice of the rock, and having renewed her youth, emerges as Bride, the fair young goddess at the touch of whose wand the dun grass turns to vivid green starred with the white and yellow flowers of spring.

Here we have what appears to be a dual goddess, and a similar duality is expressed in the traditional Gaelic concept of the sun as having two seasons—the time of the Big Sun and the time of the Little Sun. These seasons were separated by the great feast days of Beltane and Samhain, which today we know as and Halloween. Given the virtually universal human experience of having an early foundation mythology to explain the creation of the seasons, the weather, the formation of the land, and so forth in terms of a Goddess, we appear to be dealing with a very ancient motif.

The story of the *cailleach* going to the well was known in specific locations. Ruth and Frank Morris, in their *Scottish Healing Wells*, mention a local version of the story on Caird's Hill, near Forres, in the heart of the Scots-speaking north east. This surviving tradition underlines the reality that, as with all mythological ideas in preliterate societies, tales were told in specific locations to make them meaningful to the local population.

The idea that Bride used a wand to turn the dun grass green is also reminiscent of the wand of the *cailleach*, of which Donald Mackenzie tells us in *Scottish Folk Lore and Folk Life*; but where Bride used hers to bring new life, the *cailleach* used hers to hammer cold and frost into the land. This echoes the underlying duality of Bride and the *cailleach*, which is itself reflective of life and death, day and night, summer and winter, and perhaps of positive and negative, north and south.

This potential polarity that further evidence links Bride and the *cailleach*—a polarity that exists in the contemporary Scottish landscape—has much to tell us. In *The Pagan Symbols of the Picts*, I have drawn attention to a range of sites in Scotland that by their very form—breast-shaped hills, in particular—appear to have become the *foci* of belief in a goddess figure. The *cailleach*, of course, is associated with many of Scotland's most prominent mountains, and there appears to be a widespread sense that the land itself was perceived to be the body of the goddess. The very name of the mountain range south of Ben Nevis, the Mamores, which is itself associated with both the *cailleach* and Bride, is derived from *mam*, a breast-shaped hill; and across Scotland, the various *paps* and *ciochs* (both alluding to breasts) are examples of this. The term *cailleach* means "the veiled one" and this is a fair description of many of our hills and mountains much of the time. However, there are other instances in the landscape that refer directly to Bride and the *cailleach*, and directly reflect this duality/polarity.

On the island of Arran at the head of Glen Sannox, there is Ceum na Caillich, which means "the step of the *cailleach*," while on the other southern side of the glen is Cioch-n-h-Oighe, which means "the breast, or nipple, of the maiden." This echoes the relationship in Scots-speaking tradition of the *carlin* (old woman or hag) and the maiden, which is precisely the same as that of the *cailleach* and Bride. The *cailleach* place name here is to the north and the maiden to the south. In the Trossachs, one of the highest mountains is Ben Ledi, often translated as the Hill of God. On its summit is an outcrop of rock called Cnoc a Cailleach; below it, on the other side of Loch Lubnaig, is a very early church site dedicated to Bride. Here, the *cailleach* reference is high in the landscape, and Bride low.

On the Island of Jura we see something a little different. Jura lies to the south of the Corryvreckan whirlpool, which is where the *cailleach* was believed to wash her plaid at the end of summer; it is of some note that this is the third biggest whirlpool in the world. Near the southern end of Jura is Craigshouse Bay, which has as its northern end Eilean Bhride (the island of Bride), while at its southern send is Rubha Caillich (the point of the *cailleach*). We would perhaps expect the *cailleach*, with her associations with winter, to be to the north, but here she is to the south (the relationship with Bride is essentially the same, though here reversed). Jura, of course, has the three Paps of Jura, which from most angles are seen as a pair; they have their own specific *cailleach*, and powerful female references, in story and place names.

Another interesting duality shows up in the far southwest. Here, on the Rhinns of Galloway, we have the interestingly named Calliness Point. While linguists continue to reject any possible link between the *cailleach* and Calanais, the name does suggest the possibility. Close to the point itself, we have a stone circle, a prehistoric mound, and the very interesting name, Kirkmaiden. The conjunction of the possible reference to a *cailleach*, or *carlin* in Calliness, and the name Kirkmaiden is possibly another example of this duality.

One other intriguing location is on the side of Bishop Hill overlooking Loch Leven in Fife. Just to the south of the breast-shaped West Lomond Hill—which, with its sister, East Lomond Hill, form the Paps of Fife—is a singular stone pillar. This is Carlin Maggie, a local witch said to have been turned to a pillar by the devil. This striking monolith has its own duality. Approached from the south, it appears to be obelisk-like; but passing to the west of it, you suddenly see that its shape is bulbous in a way that is strongly reminiscent of the Neolithic Venus figures found in many parts of Europe. The Ordnance Survey also marks the spot as being the Carlin and her Daughter, a possible reference to a smaller pillar, closer into the cliff face, just behind Carlin Maggie. Given that, on West Lomond Hill we have a non-defensive raised area called Maiden Castle; and to its north west, at the bottom of a steep incline, we have the Maiden Bore, a site of fertility rituals in the past; it is perhaps worth thinking here of the conflation of "daughter" and "maiden"—and, given the parallels with Gaelic traditions, even Bride herself.

Another intriguing piece of information comes from Sanquhar in the southwest. Here, at Bride's Well, it was a May Day custom to put nine white stones in the well in honor of the saint. This harks back to ancient Beltane rituals. Mackinlay, in his *Folklore of Scottish Lochs and Springs*, tells us that there were wells, usually healing ones, dedicated to Bride in the counties of Dumfries, Peebles, Lanark, Renfrew, Dumbarton, Perth, Fife, and Aberdeen. Healing wells, in many instances, seem to have been in use in pre-Christian times, and in some parts of Scotland there are well rituals that appear never to have ceased; the best known of the Scottish healing wells is the Clootie* Well on the Black Isle. Again, this underlines the indigenous nature of the Scottish Bride.

There are dozens of Bride place names all over Scotland, including many Kilbride and Kirkbride forms, which reinforce the early Christian use of the persona they developed. Just off Kilmartin Glen, which is in its entirety a sacred landscape, in a small side glen is the pre-Reformation site of Saint Bride's Chapel. It is close to cup- and ring-marked rocks and a nearby chambered cairn. The immediate Kilmartin area contains extensive megalithic sites, including observation alignments for solar eclipses and the nineteen-year moon standstill. This was a location of major importance five thousand years ago. On the east coast there are several interesting Bride locations in Angus that clearly predate the arrival of Christianity. In Glen Clova, in the Angus foothills of the Grampian mountains, there is a now-overgrown pool by the roadside, just east of the Gella bridge, called Bride's Coggie. *Coggie* is an old Scots term for "a wooden bucket," and this pool is said to be stone lined.

In the same area, place names that refer to women might give weight to the idea of a goddess site here. There is Clachnabrain, which comes from the Gaelic *clach-na mnathan* (the stone of the women), and Braeminzeon, which is *braigh na mnathan* (hillside of the women). Nearby was the first location of a church in the glen. In a story that is

---

* Editor's Note: *Clootie* means "rag." Clooties would be tied to a tree near a healing well, with a prayer for Brigit's/Bridget's help, as part of a healing ritual; hence, clootie well and clootie tree.

repeated throughout the country, we are told the stones of the church were always moved overnight from the selected spot till the site itself was changed. And it seems possible that the name of the glen, Clova, is a goddess name akin to Clota, an early name for the River Clyde. It is perhaps worth noting that, in this section of the glen, adders are regularly seen. In a glen just a few kilometers to the east, Glenesk, there is another Bride name, which this time is Bride's Bed and refers to an ancient human-made circular depression below Craigmaskeldie at the head of the glen, through which a stream runs. Also in Angus, to the south at Kingennie, near Dundee, there is Bride's Ring, the remains of a prehistoric defensive structure. These sites are all prehistoric.

In *The Pagan Symbols of The Picts*, and elsewhere, I have put forward the suggestion that, in pre-Christian Scotland, there was a concept of a dual goddess figure surviving in Gaelic tradition as the *cailleach* and Bride, and in Scots as the carlin and the maiden. What the evidence clearly shows is that Bride is an indigenous figure, similar to the figure underlying the Irish Saint Bridget, but not developed from her. This Scottish Bride, who in later Gaelic tradition is spoken of as the birthmaid of Christ, as she was said to have been present at his birth, appears to have deep roots indeed. The fact that Scotland's contemporary landscape contains so many references to Bride and the *cailleach*, and that sites such as the Paps, which provide clusters of different types of evidence suggesting sanctity, I suggest, makes clear that there was a distinct indigenous mythology in pre-Christian Scotland in which Bride played a central role. In terms of the recent archaeological discoveries at Ness of Brodgar, which show sophisticated ritual activity and extensive megalithic construction long before the erection of Stonehenge or the pyramids, we might consider whether the functionaries here and elsewhere were focused on a female-centric religion, and whether indeed those functionaries themselves were men or women.

REFERENCES:

Bede, The Venerable. 1955. *The History of the English Church and People*. Penguin: London.

Campbell, E. 2000. "Were the Scots Irish?" *Antiquity*. 75: 285–292.

Carmichael, Alexander. 1994. *Carmina Gadelica*. Edinburgh: Birlinn.

Leslie, Jhone. 1888–95. *Historie of Scotland 8 vols*. Edinburgh: Blackwood.

McHardy, Stuart. 2003. *The Quest for the Nine Maidens*. Edinburgh: Luath.

—2012. *The Pagan Symbols of the Picts*. Edinburgh: Luath.

Mackinlay, J. M. 1893. *Folklore of Scottish Lochs and Springs*. Glasgow: Hodge.

Mackenzie, D. A. 1935. *Scottish Folklore and Folk Life*. Glasgow: Blackie.

McNeill, Marion. 1959. *The Silver Bough*. Glasgow: MacLellan.

Morris, F. and R. Morris. 1982. *Scottish Healing Wells*. Sandy: Althea Press.

Ross, Anne. 1992. *Pagan Celtic Britain*. London: Constable.

The First Keening

Valerie Freseman

So they sent a man of them to spy out the battle and the actions of the Tuatha dé*, namely, Ruadan son of Bres and of Brig the Dagda's daughter. For he was a son and grandson of the Tuatha dé. Then he related to the Fomorians the work of the smith and the wright and the brazier and the four leeches who were around the well. He was sent again to kill one of the artisans, that is Goibniu (the smith). From him he begged a spear, its rivets from the brazier and its shaft from the wright . . . Now after the spear had been given to him, Ruadan turned and wounded Goibniu. But Goibniu plucked out the spear and cast it at Ruadan, so that it went through him, and he died in the presence of his father in the assembly of the Fomorians. Then Brig came and bewailed her son. She shrieked at first, she cried at last. So that then was the first time crying and shrieking (keening) was heard in Ireland.

~ Cross and Slover, *Ancient Irish Tales*, 1936

Woe, woe, woe to me,
Oh grief at the night and the morning.
Where is he that tore a river from my eyes?
My son shall no more see morning.

---

* Editor's Note: The Tuatha dé were an ancient race in Irish mythology. Brigit was said to be the daughter of the Dagda, the good god of the Tuatha dé, and wife of Bres, king of the Fomorians, another ancient race with whom the Tuatha dé were often at odds.

Woe, woe, woe to me,
Grief at the night and the morning.
Why was he sent, a spy to his own?
Our kings are thieving the mothers.

Woe, woe, woe to me,
Grief at the night and the morning.
What song did it sing, what shriek from arrow did ring?
Oh glory, vain glory, has sung it.

Woe, woe, woe to me,
Grief at the night and the morning.
Where blows the east? Where blows the south?
The ashes of conflict have born me.

Woe, woe, woe to me,
I'll shriek at the day till he comes.
They tell me he's gone, gone to glory
I forge tears for my dear one in vain.

Woe, woe, woe to me,
Grief at the night and the morning.
Daughters, sisters, wives and lovers,
We search out the fallen together.

Woe, woe, woe to me,
What wave now breaks over the battle?
No swelling of seas, no trembling of rain,
Tears cannot heal the land from this pain.

Woe, woe, woe to me,
There is light at the dawn, and warmth in the dark.
I sing, I wail, to make you whole.
Oh, comfort us, voice of *Bean Caoinadh*!

Brigit's Runes in Sweden:
The Völva and the Sun
Kirsten Brunsgaard Clausen

"Brigit is here, Brigit is here!" The children in Gaelic-speaking areas still merrily announce her coming to this day. It is the morning of February 2. Icy cold. Earth is frozen deep. The landscape black, white, grey. No life. The world is dreaming, still, and deep. *Cailleach*, the wise mother, has reigned throughout the winter; now even her time has come to pass on. On every hearth the fire is put out, the last glow cooling to coal and ashes. Silence.

That is the time when she comes! Newborn from the wells in the green woods, She comes walking, accompanied by her white cow. Our life-giving mother, the sun. She is all dressed in white, a long red ribbon around her waist and the golden star of the sun on her chin. Where she walks, the land becomes green in her footsteps. She promises light, warmth, and abundance to all. New fires are now happily lit in every home.

Let me tell you of my journey with this goddess. In 2006, on an excursion to a large bronze-age rock art site near Norrköping in Sweden, we stepped over a rune inscription with six letters, overgrown, unknown. It said: BRAIDO. "A goddess," said the guide. Puzzled, we ran through all the Nordic goddesses who were familiar to us—Freya, Siv, Idun, Urd. Braido we had never heard of!

The renowned archaeologist, Arthur Nordén, wrote in 1925: " . . . BRAIDO, meaning The Exalted One, could be some local witch." He dated the runes to 200–400 CE, saying "this means that they are extremely unique and so ancient that rune writing in Scandinavia cannot be dated any earlier." More recent examinations agree on the dating. The name ending with an –o is the ancient feminine, today turned into –a (Swedish) or –e (Danish), yielding Braida or Braide.

A great and exalted goddess, Braido seems to have been similar to such other high Scandinavian goddesses as Völva and Gydia. Völva was the seeress, while Scandinavian Gydia/Gyda seems to be equivalent to the Greek goddess Pythia, meaning "high priestess" or "shaman." Who wiped her out of our knowledge? This was the question that started me off on my journey to trace her background.

We know first of all that, at around the time these runes were made, war-like people arrived in Scandinavia and seem to have destroyed the old culture. They started building small family houses instead of long-houses, and they introduced war, patriarchy, aristocracy, and the subordination of women. They did not come in peace.

I knew how, in Scandinavia, first, the Aesir-religion and, later, Christianity usually treated old deities: killing them by silence, demon-izing them, or, if they were too popular, turning them into subordinate wives of gods or into Christian saints. In my journey, I first went to Britain, as we have no saints left in Sweden. In Britain, even today, we find the highly honored and most beloved Saint Bridget. The stories of well-dressings, the connection between Saint Bridget and the white cow, the ever-flowing milk and abundance whisper to us and disclose a figure presumably much older than Christianity: Braid, the Bride of Spring, in a new guise.

At the end of a traditional Irish Brigit ceremony, the older women put a little white wand into the Bride doll's hand. In Scandinavia, the staff or wand is the attribute of the Völva, the shaman, who was con-nected to the tree of life, the *axis mundi*, and the life-creating forces. The Nordic word *volr* means staff, and thus the Völva is "the staff-bearer." Today, the staff has become the magic wand in Disney films, but even bishops and kings still carry them as signs of dignity. In archaeological excavations in Scandinavia, the staff next to the buried woman is found in several graves containing great riches, such as the Oseberg Ship.

Brigit is a goddess of fire—protector of cooking, bread-making, and smith-craft, and allied to inspiration, poetry, and consequently to oracle, *seid*, and shamanism. As life-giver and sustainer, she is connected with midwifery, healing, and plant medicine.

She is also connected to spinning and weaving. The verb *braid* means to weave and plait, and tradition says that Brigit originally taught women how to spin and weave. Brigit, like the Norns, even spun the threads of life, intertwined them, bound them together—in friendship, and all kinds of good relationships. So the maiden Braido has the fullest potential of life-giving, and possesses the greatest mysteries of the life force, as does every young maiden. She surely is the "The Exalted One," as Arthur Nordén wrote in 1925.

After tracing her abroad from Britain to France and Germany, where various traditions have also carried forth surviving fragments of her story, I started off by finding parallels and associations in fragments of Brigit in our Nordic tradition.

The Nordic word for healing, *helbrejda / helbräjda / helbrede*, discloses Braido as meaning "to become whole (*hel*) again with the help of Braido (*brejda*)." I found huge Braid stones (Braido-sten and Brudsten, Gotland), Bride Mountains (Brudberg), and various local names and places. In Nordic mythology, I found her home, Braida-Blick. The myth says, "... then there is also this place called Braida-blick (Bride-gleaming), and there is nowhere a fairer dwelling." Into this place the later Aesir gods, Balder and Nanna, moved once she had vanished.

I found children's nursery rhymes in both Danish and Swedish, beautifully disguising her. Mothers might have been able to pass on their knowledge to the next generation camouflaged in tales and rhymes, and little girls were not subjected to the Church's magnifying glass, searching for heathendom and heresy.

Imagine my astonishment when I one day caught sight of our Lucia and really saw her, as for the first time. Lucia is the most beloved of all traditional collective Swedish figures, outshining both Father Christmas and Jesus. As mentioned earlier, we have no saints in Sweden, but when this young woman with her maidens (nineteen, or the amount you may be able to summon) slowly comes walking into your totally dark bedroom, the city hall, or church before dawn on a starry black and ice-cold December morning, all dressed in white, with a long red ribbon around her waist, and bringing forth the light in a huge crown with tall burning candles on her head, singing her promises of peace and joy, not a single eye is dry. It does not matter how many times in your life you witness a Lucia morning, you will weep for joy and beauty every time. Everyone is touched deeply in their hearts by the symbol of a young woman bringing light and hope into the dark, whatever aspect in their life it may touch.

In her arms, Lucia carries a huge basket with Lucia buns. Remember that Brigit brought abundance; the Lucia buns are swastika in shape (the clockwise, Bronze Age sun symbols), looking very like the Brigit's crosses in straw that are still being made on Imbolc in Ireland. They are yellow, sun-colored buns, rich with expensive saffron, and filled with raisins, butter, and almonds. And with her come nineteen maidens. Catching sight of her, I suddenly realized that this was actually Braido still coming!

Considering that in Britain and Ireland, because of her popularity, Brigit could not be subdued and thus was converted into the Christian Saint Bridget, one might guess there was a similar process in Scandinavia. As the Church could not get rid of our Braido, they might at one point have accepted facts and made a quick decision to keep her, but transformed her into a harbinger of "Christ, the light of the world" instead of the bringer of spring. They might have clapped their hands on finding an insignificant and unknown Italian saint, who had nothing to do with Sweden, but who happened to bear the name Lucia, meaning "light." No scholar has been able to give a satisfying and trustworthy explanation as to how this minor Italian saint came to play such a significant role in Swedish tradition. And thus they succeeded in converting Braido into a Christian, changing both her name to Lucia and her place in the calendar from February to Christmas, and dressing her in a new story—Lucia's martyr story—and the thing was settled: Braido could stay, thoroughly disguised.

Around 200–400 CE, women at the old cult mound near Norrköping carved six runes in the rock beside the huge area of holy Bronze Age rock art. They did not write them in coal, nor did they cut them in wood. They carved them into the mountain. They are the only runes of such a high age in Scandinavia, unknown and unattended until a few months ago. Now, they have been repainted red again and may be found as Östergötlands

Runinskrifter, carved from the right side—ODIARB—and mirrored, both of which were common at that very early time of rune-writing.

The war people had come by the time that the runes were carved. These people were glorifying violence in a way never heard of before, honoring the merits of young men murdering on the battlefield, over the traditional merits of old women's wisdom of life. At some point, the old women at the cult mound might have come fully to realize that the times had changed forever, and their own time and traditions were over. Maybe they were under threat, or perhaps most of the tradition bearers were already slain, when somebody made her way to the ancient mound one night and, in the flickering light of a torch, did the only thing left to do— put her name into stone to show those who came after that surely she, the lovely, life-giving goddess, the great Braido, once was here.

Without the testimony those old women left us, today we would have had a hard time verifying that Braido was very present here in Scandinavia. Thanks to these women's courage, determined will, devotion, and sense of responsibility, we can see that it is very likely that she was here. And thanks to women throughout all time, who kept honoring Brigit in the Isles, telling stories of her in Europe, and celebrating Lucia in remote parts of Sweden, we may put together a picture of her: Braido, the maiden of abundance, the most beloved giver of light and life, and a profound model of the full potential in every young woman today.

REFERENCES:

Burenhult, Göran. 1991. *Arkeologi i Norden 1.* Stockholm, Sweden: Natur och Kultur.

—1991. *Arkeologi i Sverige.* Höganäs, Sweden: A. B. Wiken.

—1988. *Länkar till vår forntid.* Stockholm, Sweden: Bonniers Förlag.

Gimbutas, Marija. 1989. *The Language of the Goddess.* London: Thames & Hudson.

—2001. *The Living Goddess.* Berkeley: University of California Press.

Gunnarsson, Ruth. 1975. *Vore gamle kalenderdage.* Copenhagen, Denmark: Lademannm.

Højrup, Ole. 1977. *Landbokvinden.* Århus, Denmark: Aarhuus Stiftsbogtrykkerie.

Høst, Anette. 2005. *Jorden sjunger.* Finland: W. S. Bookwell.

Jones, Kathy. 2002. *The Ancient British Goddess.* Glastonbury: Green Magic.

—1990. *The Goddess in Glastonbury.* Glastonbury: Ariadne Publications.

Liljenroth, Gunnel & Göran. 1995. *Hel, den gömda gudinnan.* Lidköping, Sweden: AMA-förlag.

—2004. *Hel i finska språket.* Lidköping, Sweden: AMA-förlag.

Lund, Troels. 1914. *Dagligdag i Norden.* Copenhagen, Denmark: Gyldendalske Boghandel, Nordisk Forlag (Bd VI).

Macalister, R. A. Stewart. 1941. *Lebor Gabála Érenn.* Dublin: Irish Texts Society.

Nordén, Arthur. 1925. *Sägen och fornminne i fiskebybygden.* Norrköping, Sweden: Fiskeby Aktiebolag.

—1936. *Norrköpingsbygdens Hällristningar*. Stockholm, Sweden: W&W.

Olsen, Harald. 2002. *Keltisk kristendom*. Stockholm, Sweden: Verbum.

Ryd, Yngve. 2005. *Eld*. Stockholm: Natur och Kultur.

Sturlasson, Snorre. "Gylfaginning," *Prose Edda*.

—"Snorres Edda och Heimskringla."

Sæter, Gjertrud, and Gro Steinland. 1996. *HUN – en antologi om kunskap fra kvinners liv*. Oslo, Norway: Spillerom.

SAINT BRIGIT

Saint Bridget's Day

Matthew Geden

Already there's a spring in my step;
touch by touch the frost disappears
in the slow light, inches into nothing.

I have given away my past,
my jumpers, books, letters and gold.
Sent them to the poor and overseas.

May they travel well, make
a difference like a smile, small
comforts, silent breaking of the soil.

Generosity has its own rewards; baby
talk, the prayers of blacksmiths, midwives,
watermen, scholars, travelers and poets.

Take what you need; flour, milk, my quill.
When the days stretch, I'll head for the hills.

BRIDGET AND KILDARE
Sister Rita Minehan

Who was this woman Bridget, who occupied and continues to occupy such an important place in the hearts and devotions of the people of Ireland? Bridget's origins are wrapped in a shroud of mystery, and the more one tries to unravel the mystery, the more the mystery deepens. Historically, very little is known about this popular saint. Folklore, story, myth, legend, poetry, hagiography, and topography abound in relation to Bridget. These sources have a symbolic significance that can lead one to very deep truths. The Irish psyche is a storehouse of such treasures. The writers of the early *Lives of the Saints* focused more on the wonders and miracles wrought by the particular saint than on the historical facts. The *Vita Brigitae: Life of Brigid*, written by Cogitosis—who may have been a Brigidine monk in Kildare in the latter half of the 7th century—is the earliest surviving written record of the tradition, writes Connolly. In the *Life*, the main emphasis is on Bridget's faith, her healing powers, her skill with animals, her hospitality, her generosity, and, especially, her concern for the poor, the oppressed, or the embarrassed.

To understand Bridget, the Christian saint, one needs to look briefly at the ancient beliefs that prevailed in Ireland prior to the coming of Christianity. Male and female deities, one of which was Brigit, were revered and worshipped in ancient Ireland. A great cult surrounded her. She is associated in Irish folklore and literature with the gifts of poetry, healing, and smith-craft, and is also associated with nature, fertility, and fire. With the coming of Christianity to Ireland, the power of these ancient beliefs began to wane. Christianity slowly took root, assimilating features of the older beliefs and practices, including, for example, the use of sacred wells, the Celtic celebration of Imbolc, and the use of fire. It was at this time of transition that the historical Bridget of Kildare was born. Bridget the saint inherits much of the folklore associated with the goddess Brigit, a dimension that contributes to her popularity. It may be an exercise in futility to try to separate the historical Bridget from the goddess since, clearly, according to Ó Duinn, the two are so interwoven. Saint Bridget stands at the meeting of two worlds. Neither the boundaries of Christianity nor the older beliefs can contain her exclusively.

There are many stories and legends relating to Bridget's birth and early years. Bridget, we are told by Paterson, was born around 453 CE. Although one story suggests Faughart, County Louth, as her place of birth, there is a strong local tradition in Kildare that Bridget was born in Umeras, about five miles northwest of Kildare town. Her father, Dubthach, was a local chieftain whose descendants may now be called Duff or Duffy. Her mother, Broicsech, was a bondmaid in Dubthach's household, and tradition holds that she was a Christian.

It is generally accepted that Bridget established her abbey and church in Kildare around 480 CE, on the site now occupied by Saint Bridget's Cathedral. MacAlister and also Pollard suggest that her foundation may have evolved from a sanctuary of Druidic priestesses who converted to Christianity.

It seems that Bridget held a unique position in the early Irish Church and the society of her day. As Abbess, she presided over a local church of Kildare and was a leader of a double monastery of men and women, Ryan tells us. Tradition suggests that she invited Conleth, a hermit from Old Connell near Newbridge, to assist her in Kildare. Her abbey was acclaimed as a center of education, culture, worship, and hospitality in Ireland, and far beyond, up to the suppression of abbeys in the 16th century.

Nothing remains today of the original Brigidine church and abbey, which were probably constructed of timber or of mud and wattle. They were pulled down, rebuilt, and enlarged many times as numbers grew in the double monastery for men and women. Cogitosus, according to Patterson, described a remarkable building in the 7th century:

The church contains the glorious bodies of Conleth and Brigid, resting in monuments which are placed on the right and left of the decorated altar, and which are adorned with various ornaments of silver and gold . . . One partition, decorated and painted with figures and covered with linen hangings, extends across the whole breadth of the other . . . Through the door on the right side the bishop entered the sanctuary, accompanied by his regular school. . . Through the other door enters the abbess with her nuns.

The abbey was ravaged and plundered on numerous occasions by the Danes and Irish alike between 835 and 998 CE, and was destroyed many times by fire.

There is no record of the Brigidine abbeys from the 16th to the 19th century. On February 1, 1807, Daniel Delaney, Bishop of Kildare and Leighlin, restored a Sisterhood of Saint Bridget to Ireland when he gathered six women catechists in Tullow, County Carlow. The Brigidine Annals, according to O'Riordan, record that Bishop Delany was not founding a new congregation but, rather, restoring "the ancient Order of Bridget." As if to show continuity between the old and the new, the Bishop brought an oak sapling from Kildare and planted it on the convent grounds. A mighty oak tree still stands as an enduring testimony to the foundation. In 1992, two sisters of Saint Bridget, Mary Minehan and Phil O'Shea, came to live in Kildare and opened a small center for Celtic Spirituality, in the spirit of Bridget of Kildare. They live in Solas Bhride, (Bridget's light), 14 Dara Park. An outreach community of women and men who call themselves Cairde Bhride (friends of Bridget) developed around the Solas Bhride Center; inspired by the values of Bridget, they work together to promote justice, peace, and reconciliation.

"Brigit's fire," a perpetual flame, burned in Kildare in pre-Christian times and was kept alight by Bridget and her nuns, possibly up to the 16th century. It was relit in 1993 by Mary Teresa Cullen, the then-leader of the Brigidine Sisters, in Market Square, Kildare, at the opening of a justice and peace conference. The conference, entitled Bridget: Prophetess, Earthwoman, Peacemaker, was organized by Afrl (Action from Ireland), a justice, peace, and human rights group, to celebrate the 10th anniversary of its Saint Bridget's Peace Cross Project. The relighting of the flame/fire seems to have caught the imagination of people all over the world. Since then, the Brigidine Sisters in Kildare are honored to be the keepers of the flame at Solas Bhride.

The day is eagerly awaited when Bridget's fire will be perpetually kept alight in Kildare. The "embers to enflame the future" are, meanwhile, being carefully tended and rekindled, Corrigan assures us.

An annual Féile Bríde, which precedes Bridget's feast day on the first of February, evolved from the 1993 Conference. Féile Bríde is a five day event jointly organized by the Brigidine sisters, Cáirde Bhride, and AfrI. It includes a pilgrimage and a peace and justice conference as core components—the secular and sacred are intertwined. There is something for everybody: local school children dramatize the legends of Bridget, and Bridget's crosses are woven by young and old. The celebration of the Eucharist and other creative rituals are conducted in the local churches and at Saint Bridget's Well.

Rituals and prayer stones at Saint Bridget's Well are changed for different occasions. Sometimes the customs associated with Saint Bridget are retold at each stone, for instance the custom of the *brat Bríde* (Bridget's mantle/cloth). On Saint Bridget's eve, it was customary to place a piece of cloth or ribbon outside the house. The general belief was that Saint Bridget's spirit traveled across the land, and she left her curative powers on the brat Bríde. It was then used throughout the year as a cure for sickness and as protection against harm, according to Ó hÓgáin.

Artists entertain those who come with a feast of poetry, music, song, and *ceili* (Irish dancing). Locals and visitors explore places associated with Bridget within the local area. This sometimes includes a visit to a small village near the Curragh, called Soncroft, where stands a limestone sculpture of *Bríd* (Saint Bridget) and the children, by sculptor Annette McCormack. When Annette decided to carve a small cross on Bridget's breast, a fossil in the shape of a crescent moon came to light under her chisel in the center of the pectoral cross "releasing a million years" of record of primeval life on earth, Swain relates. Féile Bríde attracts participants from many countries. The exciting growth and success of the Féile has its source in the energy and efforts of the community from which it sprung.

Bridget is clearly a woman for our time. A worldwide resurgence of interest in all aspects of Celtic heritage is leading many individuals and groups to rediscover, reconnect with, and draw inspiration from the lives of the early Irish saints. People are looking for a spirituality that is inclusive of all creation. Saint Bridget is emerging once again at a time of transition of the universe. The wealth of stories and legends that exist about her are being retold with a new relevance, as parables for today. Looking at her life, and at some issues that confront and challenge us, it seems clearer why Bridget is being reclaimed as a model for our time.

Bridget, with her closeness to nature, was a very accessible saint to women and men. In a new hymn, she is invoked by Liam Lawton "to heal our wounds and green our Earth again." Those concerned about the environment and the future draw inspiration from the reverence and respect that she and our Celtic ancestors had for the land.

Many are reclaiming Bridget because of the significant role she, and succeeding abbesses, exercised in the Church and the society of their time. She is seen as a model of equality. Bridget was one of the founders of monastic life in Ireland, according to Mould Pouchin. And Cogitosus tells us that Bridget and Conleth "governed their primatial church by means of mutual happy alliance." In the 7th and 8th centuries, there is no doubt, the abbess of Kildare enjoyed extensive rights. She appointed not only her own bishop but also those of neighboring territories, according to Mary Condren. What emerges from the stories of Bridget's abbey is the portrait of a powerful leader, an organizer, an *anamchara* (soul friend), a healer, a prophetess. She is a potent symbol of womanhood, showing us, in so many ways, the feminine side of God.

The *Book of Lismore* refers to Bridget as the "prophetess of Christ." Compassion and a sense of justice have been distinctive characteristics of the prophetic person down through the ages. No fewer than 23 of the 32 chapters of the *Life of Brigid* have to do with her compassion and concern for the poor. Christ is seen in every person, especially in the guise of the poor person. Those concerned with justice issues are challenged by her response. A sense of justice impelled her to share: "what is mine is theirs."

Bridget is the woman who, above all others, embodies the spirit of pre-Christian Celtic and Christian Celtic Ireland, reflects Brophy. Her life inspires unity and reconciliation. In a world of much fragmentation, with many divides, there is a search for a sense of unity, a search for connection, a search for the sense of the whole family, human and natural. "In her femininity, Bridget inclusively embraces many kinds of cross currents, some of them apparently contradictory—the ancient and the new, the Pagan and the Christian, the animal and the human, the rich and the poor—and from this it is clear that her ample cloak can accommodate all apparently irreconcilable differences," says B. Monaghan, which recalls the traditional invocation, *Faoi bhrat Bhride Sinn* (May we be under the cloak of Bridget).

The stories and legends about Bridget, which depict her as a woman of energetic action, are summed up in Sellner's phrase, " . . . hers is a legacy not of words, but of a lifetime of ministry." If one, however, were to seek the source from which Bridget drew her strength and energy, one could probably find the answer in this story, recorded by Swayne:

> Saint Brendan, the Navigator, standing one day on the cliff top, watched two whales in fierce combat. Suddenly the smaller whale, with a human voice, cried out for help—not to Brendan but to Brigid, who was not even present. The cry was answered, and the combat ceased. Brendan was puzzled as to why he had been ignored. "Do you always think about God?" asked Brigid, when the two met. "Yes," replied Brendan, "except at times when my boat is caught in a storm and I am concentrating on keeping afloat." "That's the explanation," Brigid answered. "From the moment I first knew God I have never let him out of my mind and I never shall."

Christian Celtic spirituality emphasizes the immanence, the closeness of God, and connectedness of all creation. People are being drawn to explore this spirituality and, in the process, are discovering and rediscovering Bridget of Kildare. The threads of Bridget's cloak are being woven anew in Kildare as the millennium unfolds. The wind is truly "whispering from the past." Excavations are uncovering traces of its 5th and 6th century history. The fire is being kindled. Hidden wells are being reclaimed. We turn again, at this threshold time in the universe, Lawton tells us, "to dance the dance of God's own Blessed Bríd."

As the American poet Denise Levertov expressed it, " . . . So much is unfolding, that must complete its gesture . . . so much is in the bud."

REFERENCES:

Brophy, P. J. Jan. 26, 1996. "A Woman to Admire." Neenagh, County Tipperary: *The Guardian.*

Condren, Mary. 1998. *The Serpent and the Goddess: Women, Religion and Power in Celtic Ireland.* California: HarperSanFrancisco.

Connolly, Sean. 1987. "Cogitosus's Life of Brigit: Content and Value." *Journal of Royal Society of Antiquaries of Ireland,* 117.

Corrigan, K. 1996. "From the Firekeepers." Unpublished.

Lawton, Liam. 1996. "Light the Fire" (hymn). Dublin: Veritas.

Levertov, Denise. 1991. "Beginners." *In Cries of the Spirit: A Celebration of Women's Spirituality,* edited by Marilyn Sewell. Boston: Beacon Press.

MacAlister, R. A. Stuart. 1999. *Proceedings of the Royal Irish Academy,* 34C.

Monaghan, B. 1999. "*St. Brigid's Day.*" *Spirituality* (Dominican Publications) 5.

Mould Pouchin, D. 1964. *St. Brigit.* Dublin: Clonmore and Reynolds.

Ó Duinn, S. 1994. Personal communication, Celtic spirituality workshop, Áras Bríde, Kildare.

Ó hÓgáin, D. 1991. *Myth, Legend and Romance: An Encyclopaedia of the Irish Folk Tradition.* London: Ryan Publishing Company.

O'Riordan, Mary, C. S. B. 1996. *Pathfinders: The Tullow Story.* Brigidine Sisters.

Patterson, J. Dean. 1982. "Kildare: The Cathedral Church of St. Brigid." Church of Ireland: Kildare.

Pollard, M. 1988. *In Search of St. Brigid, Foundress of Kildare.* Armagh, Northern Ireland: Trimprint.

Ryan, J. 1978. *St. Brigid of Cill Dara.* Dublin: Irish Messenger Publications.

Sellner, E. 1989–1990. "Brigit of Kildare: A Study in the Liminality of Women's Spiritual Power." *Crosscurrents* Winter.

Swayne, S. 1993. *Intercom.* Dublin: Veritas.

Poem for Saint Bridget's Day

Joan McBreen

I

Children gather rushes,
wind whistles through their fingers,
rain blurs their vision;
all evening they will weave
and interweave crosses,
the history of Brigit's love.

II

It is early morning. A chieftain
slowly lifts his head, sees a woman enter
bearing armfuls of green spokes.
Her face floats
all day about him, her body's outline
vague.
He woke twice that night,
wandered to the window
tired with darkness,
unaware what had bound them
together; spring, perhaps,
the green stems,
her breath warm
on his face or their two shadows
caught in branches outside
like fish in a net.

GROWING UP WITH BRIGIT
Emily Stix

My first experience with Brigit came in my burgeoning maiden years. Upon encouragement from my ever supportive—if not motivated by his own prerogative—father, I represented Brigit in an Imbolc ceremony conducted at our local Pagan community, Circle Sanctuary. Located in rural Wisconsin, Circle's practice is to conduct group rituals in a converted barn, encourage learning about and caring for the Earth through hands-on activities, and celebrate holidays neglected by modern American society, such as May Day and, of course, Imbolc. The implications of this ritual, in which we invoked Brigit's spirit, were a bit lost to me at such a young age, but they have often resurfaced and impacted the days and years since then. From those maiden days of walking through a restored barn carrying a Brideóg, to visiting Brigit's Well in Kildare, Ireland on multiple occasions in the not-so-maiden but not-quite-mother phase of my life, I feel her encouraging, positive presence, and feel honored to call Brigit of Kildare the patron(ess) saint/goddess/ moral exemplar of my family.

The passive role I played during that Imbolc ceremony so many years ago stands in contrast to my first visit to Ireland over a decade later. During those soul-searching years that are late adolescence, I spent six months discovering for myself the better part of continental Europe and the Island. A day in Brigit's hometown of Kildare offered an especially spiritual juncture of the trip. After exploring her church and fire temple remains and performing a simple ceremony with Sisters Mary Minehan and Phil O'Shea, the nuns who work so tirelessly to preserve her memory, I journeyed to Brigit's Well with my father to scatter my Irish grandfather's ashes and honor his memory. In that moment, I felt as if I was reconnecting Grandpa Bill with Mother Earth via the well's cleansing waters, which help to sustain the country he so loved and sang about. I also felt a personal connection, not only with the land and water, but also with my dad, our entire family tree, and all the energy in the universe that is never created or destroyed. I was a part of the continuous cycle of life and death, but I duly acknowledged what a microscopic role I played in the cycle. I found myself content with these thoughts, my closest version of praying, and thanked Brigit for her energy and guidance. I was not aware I had asked a question, yet I had the peripherals of an answer.

I continued to evolve my beliefs through the next few years (a habit I do not foresee ending), searching for meaning in the answers I was formulating. Again, I traveled to Kildare, this time for the week-long Imbolc celebration. Most of the town, along with hundreds of other worshipers, participated in a night-time ceremony for Saint Bridget's Day at her well. Saint Bridget's statue at her Well was covered in flowers, while the glow of a thousand candles intensified everything around us. The energy during the pilgrimage was palpable, and I actively absorbed and added to it. We began with a procession filled with group singing and light musical accompaniment. Singing in unison with so many others who shared my wave length, while walking toward a common goal, was an incredibly loving, comfortable, and inclusive feeling. Traditional sacraments were performed, such as the blessing of her mantle and the displaying of her cross. The night ended with divinations for the year to come; mine mostly included hopes of not forgetting the magic in that moment. Through song and ritual, we invoked Brigit in a safe space as a community. My thoughts on this occasion were few; I was simply in the moment with Brigit and her followers. I felt emotions, but mostly I felt at peace.

The next day, we returned to Bridgets' Well to cut a piece of the large blue mantle, which serves throughout the year as a symbol of healing. That piece of cloth and a cross, which I learned to weave at a workshop in Kildare, currently hang above my bed as a reminder of Brigit and her constant presence and protection.

For me, no intimate experience with Brigit can be compared or tested against another. Each was intense and significant, but in profoundly different ways; I left each with a deeper sense of understanding, due to the patron saint of learning. Whether as a young girl eagerly playing a part that puts her at the center of attention, or as a young adult questioning the meaning of life, or as myself now, content with the here and the moment, Brigit is always with me, in me, and around me. Together, we are part of life's cycle from maiden to mother to crone.

Donations at Brigit's Well
The holy well at Liscannor on the Atlantic with donations and offerings.

Fire Temple Stone
The stone from the ancient Fire Temple in central Kildare.

Locals Praying

Kildare people out in Brigit's morning seeking her blessing and praying.

The *Brat* Bride

Patricia Monaghan gathering up the *brat* Bride (Brigit's cloak) in the morning after Brigit has traveled and blessed the land during the night.

Brigit of Ireland: A Historical Novel

Cindy Thomas

Always remember to forget the troubles that passed away,
but never forget to remember the blessings that come each day.

~ Old Irish Proverb

"Brigid, how did ye get away without a beating?" Cook grabbed Brigid by the arm as the two marched toward the dairy. "He can't hurt me, Cook. Not any more than he already has." Brigid wiggled free and ran ahead, her feet digging into the damp dirt path. The wind whistled past her ears, but all she heard was the sound of her mother's voice, clearer than she'd ever heard it before. "Bear up, Brigid. Take heart. Bear yer lot." What could her mother have meant?

Brigid shoved the barn door wide and flung herself onto a pile of hay. The animals' smell soothed her. They asked nothing from her, gave all they had to give, and would never take anything back. If only people were the same.

Cook marched in after her, nearly hysterical. "Why didn't you answer the master? Don't ye know, lass, we'll all suffer for it? Could ye not think about us?"

Brigid sat up, pieces of hay sticking in her hair and between her fingers. "Think of others? Is that not what I have been doing? I make sure the hungry get what they need from our dairy. I get up at dawn and return to my bed long after the chickens roost. I work for the master, not myself.

How can ye say that?" Brigid trailed off into a long sob that reached the depths of her soul.

If she had expected sympathy, she didn't get it from Cook. "'Tis time ye learned yer place, Brigid. Ye do what yer supposed to because yer a slave. 'Tis a far better lot than joining the starving masses wandering the woods with the wolves." She stomped out of the dairy and shoved the door closed, leaving Brigid alone in the dark.

"She doesn't understand," Brigid said to the cattle, the doves in the rafters, the chickens, and to God, if he was listening.

Brigid longed to stay there, with her face buried in the hay, but she felt a strange urging to return to the house and seek Dubthach's forgiveness. She hated the thought, but at the same time, she knew she had no choice. Cook was right. She was a slave, and slaves have their place. If she continued to act with disrespect, Dubthach would exact a punishment on them all, fearing some sort of rebellion. Brigid couldn't bear being the cause of it. She had to go back.

Evening had cast its black cloak. Brigid couldn't see her feet so she concentrated on making her way toward the dimly lit turf-topped house. She rammed her toe into a tree root, causing a shard of pain to shoot up her leg; but thankfully she didn't fall. When she reached the house and cracked the door open, all was quiet.

Brigid's father had wanted an explanation. She sighed, tapping her fingers on the rock wall of the kitchen. He was still sitting at the table, examining parchment record books by candlelight. He looked up at her. His jaw was set. The old man dropped his writing instrument and curled his fists into balls.

"Dare to come back, did ye?" He shoved his round gut away from the table. "I'll not have such disrespect from ye, Brigid. The others will think I favor ye simply because ye were born to me."

Brigid gulped hard. Her own hands tightened under her apron. He never favored her. Never. "I'm sorry." She hung her head to keep the repulsive man from reading her true thoughts.

Dubthach was still for a moment, then slammed his fist on the table. "Very well. I'll accept yer apology. For yer penitence, ye'll have extra chores all week."

"Aye, sir."

"But ye'll have to do something for me first. I want an answer to the question, lass. How is it ye produce so much in my dairy when others do not?"

She linked her fingers together and squeezed, bringing her hands up to her lips. "The poor will always be with us." What she said surprised her more than it did her father.

"Aye. That's what I always say." Dubthach narrowed his eyes and stared. Brigid was uncertain whether he wanted to hear the explanation or whether he just liked the calming rhythm of her voice. No matter whether it was midmorning or suppertime, the slothful man could nod off quicker than a dragonfly darts.

She began. "Well, ye do have fine animals in yer barn. God has blessed ye with that. The cows are healthy indeed." Noting that he was being lulled to sleep, she kept up her rambling. "I hear the sheep are fine specimens also. And bearing young every spring. Just yesterday, Brian said . . . " She continued her banal observations for several minutes more until Dubthach's head folded down to his chest and great breaths of air pushed through his wrinkled lips. He was asleep.

Brigid lowered herself onto a tree stump chair. Her father took pride in his possessions. For an Irishman, healthy chickens and livestock meant wealth. When things went well he was bearable, she had to admit. But life was uncertain, something a slave knew well and a *laird** only remotely understood.

If a wolf would happen to steal into the barn and kill some of the herd, Dubthach would erupt into a rage lasting longer than a December night. Wolves hunt. They eat chickens; they devour calves. Didn't the old man know that? Why should he be surprised? Did he think he could invoke some magical power to hold the forces of nature at bay?

Brigid rose and stepped away from the fire. The old man would likely doze there until dawn. She lit a twist of straw from the candle dripping on the table. She'd need a wee bit of flame to light her path to the maiden's quarters.

---

* Editor's Note: *Laird* is an old Scottish word referring to a member of the gentry.

Outside, there were no shadows, no moonlight. She heard movement near the house, but assumed the noise she heard was from the birds roosting in the oaks for the night. Brigid tiptoed, as if she feared she'd wake the fairies. Of course she didn't believe in such things, but in Ireland you had to be ready for anything. Patrick had said that, having come from a land across the Irish Sea, although Brigid didn't fully understand what he meant.

A voice from behind startled her. "Excuse me, miss. Might ye have a wee bit of food for a poor lad?"

She crouched low to the ground, as if she could hide herself. *A fairy?* Couldn't be. She managed to turn on squatted legs to see the form of a thin boy staring down at her. He came into the glow of her torch, and she saw that he was wearing tattered clothes. Wisps of raven hair stuck out beneath his gray felt cap, too large for the lad's wee head, but he was a boy just the same. Not a fairy at all.

Despite Patrick's warning, she hadn't been ready. The unexpected encounter made her search for words, stuttering in the process. She'd helped beggars before. That's what had started Dubthach's interest in how she was feeding the poor. But they had never come around in the dark of night before.

The lad's dejected, deep-sunken eyes convinced her she'd have to think of something. Whispering a quick prayer beneath her breath, Brigid ordered him to wait outside the barn door while she went searching, praying all the while.

The moon finally made an appearance, just as her torch was dying. A beam of light pushed its way in through the cracked door, illuminating the cow's mud-colored face.

"I know 'tis not time for yer milking, but supposing ye'd give me just a wee bit for the poor lad outside?"

Was that a nod from the cow or was she seeing things? Brigid ran for the wooden bucket she'd placed by the feed sacks when she milked earlier. To her delight, the cow did have more to give.

"Now what about yer chickens?" Brigid eyed the red-feathered birds who'd been disturbed by her presence. They clucked about the barn floor as if trying to avoid her suggestion.

"Come on, now. Have ye no compassion for a starving lad?"

The chickens lighted on their nests and clucked their ear-shattering agreement. "Oh, God, don't let them wake Dubthach—or worse, the foxes." Brigid retrieved two brown eggs and one white one with yellow speckles.

"Thank ye kindly, God's creatures." She put the treasures into the pocket of her apron and poured the milk into a tin dish. Then she headed carefully for the barn door, ever mindful of the gifts she held.

After squeezing through the opening, Brigid greeted the lad with the best smile she could muster. She'd better warn him. "Do not be coming here again at this hour. If the master does not chase ye away, the wolves will."

The door to the main house crashed open. "Brigid, are ye there?"

"Hurry! Don't come back!" She shooed the boy away into the woods and shuffled over to the house.

"Ye fell asleep . . . I mean ye were tired and all . . . and I thought I'd leave ye alone."

"Enough of yer rambling. Was that another beggar I saw?"

No use to pretend otherwise. "Aye."

"Tell me how ye did that trick? How ye got milk and eggs when the animals should not have had any to give?" Dubthach could see in the dark like an owl.

"'Tis not a trick. I just . . . " Brigid stumbled for the right words. Her master thought he'd found the secret to worldly wealth. How could she ever explain the wonders of God to a man like him?

He waved his cloaked arm toward the house. "Come back inside. Sit. There's a trick here and ye'll teach it to me." The round man waddled back through the oak door, barely able to squeeze his body through the opening.

She followed him inside and lit two tallow candles from the smoldering peat fire. She placed them on the table next to the candle stump left from Dubthach's earlier reading, and a circle of light filled the center of the keeping room, leaving the outer edges in darkness. *Like Patrick's message in Ireland*, she thought.

Dubthach blinked his eyes. He stood and motioned toward the cupboard. "Bring me some tea."

Brigid winced as she lifted the kettle off the iron hooks hanging over the fire. How did Cook manage? Brigid was efficient in the dairy, but the kitchen was unknown territory. She carried the hot pot over to the cupboard just as Cook bustled in the door.

"Ye'll burn yerself, darlin'. What are ye doing?"

"Getting tea for the master."

"Och! Why did ye not carry the mug over to the fire instead of the other way 'round?" She snatched the kettle from Brigid and plopped it down on the dirt floor. Then she marched to the cupboard and fetched a mug. Cook poured steaming liquid into the mug and returned the pot to the fire, refusing Brigid's offer to help.

Brigid put her hands on her hips. "I'm not a child."

Cook ignored her, served Dubthach his tea, and turned to leave. She stopped short at the door and motioned for Brigid to come near. "I'll be in the field first thing in the morning with Alana. Meet us there after yer done milking. Brian needs help with the plow."

"But what can I . . . "

"Needs lots of hands, he does." Cook winked at her.

"Fine, then."

"Now, on with it!" Dubthach raised his mug to his bristled face. "Tell me the secret."

Brigid lowered herself onto the stump seat. "Once again I coaxed extra milk and eggs from the animals in the barn, but this time there was more than enough for three."

"What? There were others with that lad? Tell me about that. How . . . ?"

"Standing near the forest's edge. I saw them when he ran away. Those pleading brown eyes and miry little faces melted my heart. They're starving, they are."

"As ye said earlier, the poor will always be around."

Why had she said that?

"Yer too soft, Brigid. Thought ye'd be more like . . . "

"Like you? Turn them away?"

He raised his hand to her. She cowered back, expecting a blow. He had never hit her, but he was an angry man and she feared him nonetheless.

He lowered his hand to his lap. His full lips turned into a grin. "Ye'll tell me the secret and I'll be patient until ye do."

"We feed the barnyard animals well. Shouldn't we also share with the poor?"

"A woman has no mind for business."

I've a mind for the Lord's business.

Brigid was tired. Her bed, and hopefully sleep, awaited her. She grabbed her cloak from a peg near the door. "Here's what I did. Here's the answer to yer question."

Dubthach wrinkled his forehead and flicked his fingers back. "Go on. Tell it now."

"I prayed. That's what I did. Here's what I said: 'Lord, what will all those hungry children eat?'" She was shouting, but she couldn't help herself. "'Can the woods bring forth enough wild berries to quiet their hungry cries? If they do have parents to feed them, I know their folks likely don't have work and will provide no more than hard biscuits. Give me a way, Lord, to help them.'"

"All those words?" Dubthach ticked off his fingers as if trying to remember exactly what she had said. "Which ones are the magic ones? Which ones make the chickens produce, the cows give more milk, make the butter sweeter and more plentiful?"

Brigid rolled her eyes and pulled the door open. "That's what I said. I'm off to my bed."

BRIDGET'S MANTLE

Bee Smith

Lay me down upon your cloak—
Swaddle me. Sing to me
your secrets of always enough.

Lay me down upon your cloak—
Wrap me snug. Tell me a story.
The miracle of always enough.

Lay me down upon your cloak—
Rock me. Gently now lay me
down in the source of always enough.

GOT MILK?:
THE FOOD MIRACLES OF ST. BRIDGET OF KILDARE

Kerry Noonan

éamus O Catháin, in discussing the connection of Saint Bridget of Kildare with cows and milk, reminds us of this traditional poem:

Oiche Shamhna gan bía
Oiche Nollag Mór gan arán
Oiche Fheile Bríde gan im
Is é sin an gearán tinn

Samhain Eve without food
Christmas Night without bread
St. Brigit's Eve without butter
That is a sorry complaint

Miracles connecting Bridget and food, especially milk, are numerous. Saint Bridget once blessed water for a sick woman, which then took on the flavor of whatever the woman desired, including milk. When caught short by visitors to her monastery, Brigit's cows could be milked three times in one day to make food for the guests. A small amount of Bridget's butter miraculously fed many guests. When Bridget wanted to give honey to a beggar, honey appeared within her house. These are just a sampling of some of the miracles performed by Saint Bridget, chronicled in the several accounts of her life written in the centuries after her death. When examining the many miracles attributed to Bridget of Kildare in these popular accounts, the predominance of miracles dealing with food or food-producing animals is striking, especially when compared to the *Lives** written about other Irish saints, or about contemporary female saints from continental Europe. What can this tell us about Bridget—both the 5th to 6th century Irish saint, and the older Celtic goddess of the same name—and about ancient Irish culture?

The *Vita Prima* of Saint Bridget, a *Life* of the Irish saint written in Latin sometime between the 7th and 9th centuries, describes an incident in which Bridget and her nuns visited Bishop Ibor during Lent in order to obtain some grain. However, Ibor had no food to offer them except pork and dry bread, presenting the nuns with a quandary: should they obey the rules of hospitality and eat the pork set in front of them, although it was forbidden to them during Lent, or should they obey the rules of the Lenten fast and refuse the meat, although this might offend their host? Bridget chose to eat the pork and not offend their host. Several of her nuns chose to abstain from it, and their pork turned into serpents on their plates. Upon seeing this, Bridget, Ibor, and the nuns fasted and prayed, and the serpents turned into pure white bread, which was then used for the Eucharist.

What are we to make of this episode? It tells us something about the politics of Irish guest-and-host relations, particularly within and between monasteries, as described by Lisa Bitel in *Isle of the Saints*. It implies that Bridget set Irish hospitality customs over Christian observance, and was rewarded by God for it. But it also illustrates Saint Bridget's concern with food—with hospitality and the female realm of food provision and processing.

The food miracles of Saint Bridget, which comprise between a third and a half of the miracles recorded in various *Lives*, are a unique indication of her sanctity, and are essential to who and what Bridget was. While many of them descended directly from the miracles performed by Christ in the Gospels, such as turning water into other beverages or multiplying existing food supplies to feed a multitude, others do not fit so neatly into this category. Caroline Walker Bynum, in *Holy Feast, Holy Fast*, discusses the religious significance of food to late medieval female mystics in their own religious imagery and in their extreme fasting behavior and

---

* Editor's Note: *Lives* here refer to hagiographies (biographies of holy people) written over centuries by a variety of authors.

food distribution, describing it as sanctification of the flesh and glorification of God, who is consumed as flesh.

However, Bridget's dealings with food were not characteristic of those 13th and 14th century fasting saints documented by Bynum, who eschewed physical food, often going so far as drinking pus or living solely on the Eucharist. Saint Bridget distributed food to the needy, as many women saints were wont to do throughout the centuries, food being the one resource that women controlled and so could distribute. Yet the kinds of food she provided, and the numerous times she did so, set her apart from this group as well. I wish here to emphasize Saint Bridget as a miraculous version of a good Irish *ban a tigh* (housekeeper). She was the apotheosis of good housewifery in her provision of abundant food for her dependents, even in the face of shortages, making her an ideal hostess. She provided miraculous solutions to common household problems, such as the feeding of unexpected guests, the replacement of lost stores, the care of milch cows and other food animals, and the successful production of dairy products. Saint Bridget's always got milk, if you need it.

Bridget's food miracles, as described in this article, are compiled from the four *Lives* at which I looked during my research: the *Life* by Cogitosus, the *Vita Prima*, the Old Irish *Bethu Brigte*, and the *Life* contained in the *Book of Lismore*. I have defined "food miracle" as a miracle that either directly affects or relates to food, or one that affects animals that produce food or will become food (such as cows and pigs). In each of these versions of Bridget's life, her food miracles are prominent. In the *Life* by Cogitosus, she performs a total of 32 miracles, 15 of which have to do with food or food-producing animals. The Old Irish *Life* describes 42 miracles, 17 of which are related to food. The *Life* contained in the *Book of Lismore* details 62 miracles, 24 of which have to do with food. The food miracles in the *Vita Prima* make up 36 percent of all the miracles. While Dorothy Bray has written about Bridget as a producer of miraculous ale, I am much more struck by the preponderance of food and hospitality miracles in general performed by the saint, and in particular the dairy miracles.

From her early childhood onward, Bridget gave food to the poor. In one instance, she was working in the dairy making butter. After dividing the yield into twelve portions (for each of the apostles) plus a larger one for Christ, she gave the butter to the poor instead of taking it into the household. When she had to bring in the fruits of her labors and had nothing to show for her work, the butter was divinely restored to her in great abundance, as Connolly, O'hAodha, and Stokes have each shown. This incident was typical of many of Bridget's miracles in that it involved not only food distribution, but also food multiplication, and dairy products. Other episodes of food distribution, from the same sources, had Bridget giving bacon intended for guests to a beggar, and apples that had been received as a gift to some lepers. The saint caused a honeycomb to appear under the floor of the home of a beggar who wished for honey.

Bridget also regularly distributed food-producing animals to the poor: she gave sheep to a boy, a cow and calf to an "unpleasant leper" (variously translated as a "haughty" leper), and she gave a cow and calf given to her by another woman, to her bishop. These latter two incidents both involve the miraculous finding of a lost calf that the saint causes to follow its mother. Food preservation was also sometimes in her power, as in the miracle of a piece of bacon, taken by a dog while Bridget was meditating, which was found uneaten and fresh a month later. Another event that might be included in this last category is the miracle of the meat thrown into the saint's cloak to be given to the poor. Instead of cooked meat, a servant mistakenly put uncooked meat into her cloak, which miraculously did not stain her mantle with blood.

These miracles all fall within the larger category of charitable alms-giving. As Bynum notes, women saints typically gave food to the poor, as women were most often in charge of food production and food preparation. This sort of distribution of food, while not exclusive to women, still made up a good deal of the charity practiced by women saints. Saint Elizabeth of Hungary's most famous miracle—that of roses substituted for the food she had intended to give away—was an indicator of this sort of charity, particularly as practiced by wealthy or noble women. While the Frankish saintly queens and royal ladies, such as Saint Radegund or Saint Clotild, also gave buildings or gold to the Church, Bridget gave cows, which indeed in Ireland at that time were considered a form of tradeable wealth, as we learn in McNamara, Halborg, and Whatley, and in Patterson. In this way, cows were both a form of wealth and a source of food, combining both sorts of charitable offerings.

Bridget also performed many miracles of food multiplication and transformation. These miracles may be read as an imitation of Christ's miracles of the loaves and fishes, or of the wedding at Cana, with Bridget standing in for the figure of Christ. She may also be considered to be imitating Mary in the latter episode, being a woman who arranged for Christ to transform food items for the benefit of humans. In direct imitation of the Cana miracle, she transformed water into ale and also into milk, stone into salt (and in one version salt into stone), meat into bread, and poisoned ale into healthful ale. On some of these occasions, she performed the transformation in order to effect the healing of a supplicant, turning water into ale for a sick woman, and water into milk for a sick nun. The miraculously transformed drink healed the sick person, as well as satisfying a craving they had.

Other transformations were intended, as in the Cana miracle, to conceal an embarrassing lack of drink or food for guests, as in the miracle of the water turned to ale in order to serve a bishop on Low Easter, or the miracle in which twelve loaves, some milk, and a lamb were sufficient to feed the companies of both Bridget and Patrick. She also covered for the neglect of one of her serving men when she caused empty vessels to fill with mead for a visiting king and his company. Just as Christ provided miraculous catches of fish for his apostles, Bridget provided a seal catch for her fisherman in order to provision some guests. Her fisherman had a harder time of it than the apostles, however—the apostles may have broken their nets under their abundant catch, but Bridget's fisherman was dragged by the seal all the way to Britain, where he spent the night, returning the next day to give Bridget and her guests their seafood.

Other multiplication miracles found in the *Lives* were not as directly modeled on Biblical precedents, being more concerned with abundance in general. Among these were the spring Brigit caused to appear in a dry land, and the bread she turned into meat. The dairy churnings that were miraculously restored to her were increased so that, from only one-and-a-half churnings, she filled many vessels with butter. One sack of malt made eighteen vats of ale. Under Bridget's supervision, the bread supply was always sufficient for her foster mother's guests. Cows gave more than their usual yield, both in the butter miracle described above and in the ability of her cows to be milked three times in a day. In the *Book of Lismore*, the additional milking of her cows in order to feed guests is recounted twice. In both incidents, the third milking was overly abundant, contrary to normal expectation. Angels told Bridget to milk the cows a third time in one episode, and the milk was not only in greater supply than previous milkings, but filled all her vessels, and went on to make a lake of milk. Bridget also restored items given to her in charity, so that the giver did not experience any lack. A woman killed her cow and burned her loom in order to feed Bridget when she was visiting. The saint restored the cow and the loom the next day, replenishing the woman's goods.

Charity was rewarded with abundance and miserliness was punished in several of Bridget's miracles. A man who refused to give her any ale from his feast in order to succor a sick woman found that all of his ale had disappeared. In the *Book of Lismore*, a woman who gave Bridget a gift of apples from her garden was angered when Bridget in turn gave them to some lepers. In return for the woman's anger, Bridget cursed her garden so that it bore no more fruit. In a similar incident from the Old Irish version of her life, Bridget not only cursed the garden of a nun who resented the saint bestowing on some lepers the gift of fruit the nun had given to Bridget, she also blessed the garden of another nun who was contented with the same charitable redistribution of her own gift of fruit to the saint. Ingratitude for charity was also punished by the saint, as in the episode in which an ungrateful leper received a cow from Bridget, but was drowned in a river because of his bad attitude, as recounted in Stokes. Celtic saints often gave way to sacred rage, which was considered one of the signs of their divine power; and true to form, Bridget's holy wrath was unleashed in these episodes.

Bridget protected crops and maintained herds, both of which were sources of food. She protected the harvest of her fields from rain, and stilled the wind and rain to protect the sheep. She maintained the number of animals in the flocks under her care, even when they had been diminished either by her own charitable giving or by theft. When thieves stole cattle under her protection, a river rose and drowned the thieves and the cattle returned to her. She also gave food to animals, as in the incidents involving dogs and bacon. Bridget even transformed wild beasts into tame, food-producing animals, and enlisted wild animals as herd dogs. Swine given to her were herded by compliant wolves, and a wild boar tamely joined her pig herd instead of dispersing it, as Connolly tells us.

All these miracles point to Saint Bridget as a provider: a generous, efficient, and miraculous manager of her household's food. Her charity, a mark of Christian piety in most saints' lives, consists mainly of food distribution, rather than other sorts of almsgiving. There *were* a few instances of her charity involving items that were not food: she gave away her father's sword, some silver vessels, and the church vestments belonging to her bishop. But mainly she gave food or cows to the poor, and hospitality to the traveler. Bridget's very words were described as food: Cogitosus, author of one of *Lives*, described them as seasoned with "divine salt."

Nor should we be surprised at the preponderance of dairy products in her miracles, since she was born when her mother had a vessel of milk in her hand, and the holy babe was washed in the new milk after her birth, according to the *Book of Lismore* and the *Vita Prima*. In the Irish folk traditions surrounding her February 1 feast day, she wandered the land with her cow the night before, blessing house and barn. In some areas, an effigy of Bridget was made out of a butter churn handle, and taken from house to house. "Milk foods and milk products, principally butter" were featured foodstuffs, O' Catháin reminds us. Kevin Danaher, in *The Year in Ireland*, states that on this feast day "butter always formed part of the meal and fresh butter was sure to be churned on the same day. The more prosperous farmer gave presents of butter and buttermilk to poor neigh-bors." Food was left out for the saint and her cow. An extra place was set at the table for passing guests. Sometimes a cloth was set out for Bridget to bless, and later this cloth was laid on the backs of cows to heal them and to ensure a good milk supply How can we explain this strong emphasis on food in both her legends and the customs of her feast day?

One possible influence has been mentioned: the relationship between female saints and food, as Bynum has highlighted, for medieval women saints in the 13th and 14th centuries. Although Bynum's study is useful in thinking about the religious meanings of food for women in the high Middle Ages, her examples, drawn from late medieval saints engaged in extreme fasting, do not explain Saint Bridget and her miracles of abundance. Bridget was not described as engaging in habitual abstinence from food. However, she was described as abstaining from food in a few interesting incidents. These seem to have involved the refusal of impure food or the exchange of supernatural foods. As a baby, Brigit would not eat the Druid's food. Instead, she was provided with the milk of a white, red-eared cow. Animals with this coloring were usually associated with the otherworld or the supernatural in Celtic myth, as Ford attests. This incident appears to have involved an exchange of one form of supernatural food for another, almost like the pork-to-snake-to-Eucharist exchange in the miracle previously described. In another episode of fasting, Bridget refused to eat the food of a heathen man who had invited her into his house, until he was converted. Both the Druid and the heathen man were converted because of her holiness immediately after her refusal to eat their food. Yet these cases appear to have more in common with the Irish custom of "fasting to distrain" (that is, to discourage or change someone's behavior, rather like Gandhi) than with the extreme religious fasts undertaken by women saints of the 13th and 14th centuries.

Is there a parallel emphasis on food found in the "lives" of female saints who were Saint Bridget's contemporaries? Looking at some continental saints of roughly the same time period as Bridget might shed some light on these food miracles. Saint Genovefa of Gaul, too, transformed water into alcoholic drink, and saved the harvest in her fields from rain. She also distributed food to the needy. However, the majority of her miracles had nothing to do with food. She was, however, described as practicing austerities, including fasting, in ways that Bridget was not. In fact, her most famous miracle, turning Attila the Hun aside from Paris, was accomplished through fasting.

After reading the *Lives* of Bridget, it is remarkable to note the comparative lack of food-related miracles in Genovefa's *Life*. Saint Radegund, a Merovingian French female saint, also performed some charitable acts of food distribution, though none of them were described as miraculous. Much of her charity consisted of giving away her jewels and gold, as well as her sumptuous clothing, rather than her food. She performed only one food multiplication miracle, in which she gave drinks of wine to those in need from a small cask that never emptied. She, like later female saints, assiduously engaged in periods of fasting and, even when not fasting, ate very abstemiously. Unlike Bridget, she did not continuously perform miracles to provide food for her convent, her guests, or the poor.

But perhaps we can find counterparts to Bridget's preoccupation with food in the *Lives* of other Irish saints. According to Dorothy Bray's *List of Motifs in the Lives of the Early Irish Saints*, Saint Patrick did perform some food miracles, but nowhere near the number performed by Bridget. The percentages of food miracles in the five Lives of Saint Patrick are: 8 percent, 16 percent, 19 percent, and 29 percent. The percentages of food miracles in the four *Lives* of Saint Bridget are: 36 percent, 39 percent, 41 percent, and 47 percent. Only two of Saint Patrick's miracles had to do with dairy products, and in those cases he was not turning stone to cheese, but cheese to stone. Adomnán's *Life* of Saint Columba contains descriptions of 118 miracles, only 11 of which had to do with food.

Saint Ita, called a "second Bridget," was not known for her food or dairy miracles. However, she was associated with a kind of miraculous milk: in the poem *Iusucán*, her prayer for the favor of nursing the Christ child at her breast was granted, and she extolled both his beauty and her joy at nursing him from her virgin breasts. As she was the foster mother of many young male saints, this nursing imagery is rather appropriate for her role in the Irish Church, yet not comparable to Bridget's miracles. Several male saints were miraculously nursed by a doe, but this did not mean they performed many food or animal miracles later in life.

If Bridget does not quite fit into Bynum's model of the medieval female saint, and did not greatly resemble some of her own contemporaries, where does the particular treatment of food in her *Lives* come from? Two possibilities suggest themselves: one is the conflation of Saint Bridget with an earlier Celtic goddess who was concerned with fertility, and another is the native Irish tradition regarding food and hospitality. Scholars such as Mac Cana, Charles Plummer, and R. A. S. Macalister have described Saint Bridget as a Christianization of a prior Irish or even pan-Celtic goddess, probably called Brigit or Brigantia, and have cited evidence from continental Celts, as well as Irish and British sources. The existence of literary sources that mentioned a figure called Brigit, who was the daughter of the mythic figure The Dagda, gives weight to this theory. Gerald of Wales' description of the perpetual fire at the convent at Kildare, tended by the nineteen virgins, seems to reveal survival of pre-Christian practices into the Christian era, as Kenney has theorized. In the 10th century, Cormac mac Cuillenáin described her thus:

> Brigit i.e. a learned woman, daughter of the Dagda. That is Brigit woman of learning i.e. a goddess whom *filid* [poets] worshipped. For her protecting care was very great and very wonderful. So they called her goddess of poets. Her sisters were Brigit woman of healing and Brigit woman of smith-work, daughters of the Dagda from whose names among all the Irish a goddess used to be called Brigit.

Here is evidence of a goddess Brigit who ruled over healing, smith-craft, and poetic inspiration. Yet the strong emphasis in Bridget's *Lives* on her protection of herd animals and production of miraculous food may also be legacies from a goddess of fertility as well. She herself seems to be an embodiment of a supernatural cauldron of plenty, a common motif in Celtic literature and legend, and her refusal of the food of an impure man is similar to the refusal of supernatural cauldrons to boil the meat of cowards, as in the Welsh poem The *Spoils of Annwfn*. And certainly the large number of holy wells (a symbolic kind of natural cauldron) dedicated to Bridget throughout Ireland also lends credence to this claim, as well as testifying to her skill at healing. In addition, Powers Coe argues that her identity as a virgin who lived within a community of women may not just be a Christian reference:

> Classical ethnographic evidence pertaining to female religious practices, albeit spotty and not remarkably useful for gaining a precise understanding of the goddess *Briganti-/Brigit or of pre-

Christian Celtic religion, does at least establish some precedents for pagan female religious communities that were, if not always virginal, at least uni-sex: isolated, associated with oaks and the fertility of the land, and reputed to practice divination, prophecy, or other forms of magic. Macalister goes so far as to argue that the 5th/6th century Saint Bridget was a priestess of the goddess Brigit who converted to Christianity and transformed the pagan college of priestesses to a convent of nuns.

Whether this is so or not, there were manifest connections between the earlier goddess and the later saint. Both had their feasts on February 1, which is one of the pre-Christian Celtic cross-quarter feast days. Known as Imbolc or Oimelc, this feast was variously associated with the start of the lactation of the ewes and with purification. Candlemas, the Christian feast which occurs the next day, celebrates the purification of the Virgin Mary after her childbirth. Since Bridget was considered Mary's midwife in folklore tradition, as both Carmichael and O'Catháin have shown, the equation of the two feasts does not seem unnatural. Mac Cana clearly sees Saint Bridget as a continuation of the earlier goddess: "For if the historical element in the legend of St. Brighid is slight, the mythological element is correspondingly extensive, and it is clear beyond question that the saint has usurped the role of the goddess and much of her mythological tradition." Yet, although Saint Bridget performed many fire miracles, consistent with the description by Mac Cana just cited, the large numbers of food miracles with which I am concerned are not explained by her attributes as poetic inspiration, smith, or healer. These food and milk miracles can be seen as the provenance of a fertility goddess, and the saint seems to have inherited some attributes and legends associated with a goddess of cows, herds, and fruitfulness in general.

Hospitality—feeding and sheltering guests—was an important feature of the Irish social fabric. Obligations to provide hospitality were legislated in the law tracts of the 8th century CE, and the Irish patron-client system also brought with it obligations to host and feed guests. The similarity between the Roman patron-client system and the system of relationship between Christian patron saints and their followers has been remarked upon by Peter Brown. The Irish client system dovetailed neatly into this paradigm as well. In this light, the reiteration of Bridget's hospitality to her guests, to her people, in the *Lives* might have served to remind the readers or auditors of the advantages of being the client of such a patron saint.

Food is a commodity. It is one of the bases of social relationships. The importance of food in Irish culture, especially dairy products, can be seen in such Irish literary examples as the *Aislinge Meic Con Glinne*, which is almost an apotheosis of the physical and visceral aspects of "whitemeats" (dairy products) as well as other taste treats. Nevertheless, the exchange of food, while intended to cement ties and create reciprocal indebtedness, often gets out of hand. Hospitality as the duty of a host can be seen in the Irish stories of *Mac Da Tho's Pig* and *Bricriu's Feast*. In these two tales, however, the provision of food for guests does not result in harmony, as it does at Bridget's feasts. Yet the importance of the food provided for guests can be seen as a common thread.

Bitel discusses the intricate nuances of rank and status inherent in the hospitality demanded and provided by monastic communities for each other. It is no coincidence that Bridget was often confronted by unexpected guests from neighboring religious communities. The appearance of Saint Patrick and his retinue in many tales within the *Lives* of Saint Bridget was not only to show her consorting with the influential figures of her time; it also highlighted the tension and competition between Patrick's *paruchia* (network of monasteries), based in Armagh, and Bridget's, based in Kildare. This explains several of the miracles in which Bridget was able to perform a feat that Patrick could not, such as converting the man who invited them to dinner.

This competition also brought out the importance of being able to provide for important guests, even when caught unawares and understocked. Bitel remarks that, " . . . important guests enhanced the status of hosts in two ways: Hosts gained by receiving major saints as guests, and by placing such guests temporarily in a position inferior to their own." Even the literary glorification of dairy products and other foods in *Aislinge Meic Con Glinne* starts off with the failure of monastic hospitality rules. Mac Conglinne, a traveling monk, was refused proper hospitality by the monks of Corcach. He then satirized the monks, and was granted of a vision of a marvelous land of food, primarily dairy products.

Cows, milk, and milk products have been an important part of the Irish economy and food supply for centuries, and have been featured in chronicles, hagiographic writings, poems, and tales. Cows are ubiquitous in Irish tales: one only need look at the *Táin Bo Cuilinge* to see their importance as a source of wealth, status, and food. The law tracts of the early medieval period mentioned a variety of dairy products: butter and cheese were important not only locally, in each particular household, but also for their trade value. In his book about the modern-day town of Ballymenone in County Fermanagh, Henry Glassie indicates the importance of butter as a sort of social glue: "Since the flow of milk into butter was uneven from farm to farm and from time to time, butter was passed around among the neighbors as the most common counter of reciprocity, the most frequent material gift to community. It took hard work and gave an essential pleasure."

Milk itself was symbolically a female concern, a female product. If woman "is food" as Bynum contends, the most visible sign of this was the milk she herself produced. Accordingly, milk, milk products, and milk production were seen to be naturally part of women's domain. Patricia Lysaght, in "Women, Milk and Magic at the Boundary Feast of May," claims:

> Traditionally, it was the woman or women of the household, who had responsibility for milking, butter-making and associated utensils, as well as the care of milch cows especially after calving, and the calves too. In the Irish context there is abundant evidence of the importance of the woman's role in the production of dairy produce, ranging from the ancient law tracts of about the eighth century, to the personal experiences of some Irish farmers' wives in modern times. It was the woman's responsibility to ensure that there was a plentiful supply of milk and dairy produce, both for household use and, also, perhaps for the market.

If this responsibility was true of the ordinary housekeeper, how much more so for the female head of a monastic community?

Bridget's food miracles placed her at a juncture of roles: abbess and housekeeper, saint and woman, human and goddess. She was not only the point of intersection between heaven and earth, as Peter Brown tells us a saint is, but also the locus where pagan and Christian patterns intersected, and where native Irish and continental traditions met. She brought the divine into the human, and infused the human with the divine, as a good saint should, and at the same time stood in two places at one time: the pagan, Irish past and the Christian present. Bridget performed feats that no ordinary woman could: she ranged about the countryside by herself in a chariot, she was ordained as a bishop (apparently by mistake), she was in charge of both monks and nuns at her double monastery, and she performed miracles. Yet, in her food miracles, she proclaimed herself as a holy and hospitable housekeeper *par excellence*. Her stores never ran out, her butter always turned out in abundance, she cared for her cows and pigs, fed her guests, and produced marvelous amounts of the milk that has been the provenance of Irish women for so many centuries.

Need milk? No worries, Bridget's got enough for you and all who enter her domain.

REFERENCES:

Bitel, Lisa. 1990. *Isle of the Saints: Monastic Settlement and Christian Community in Early Ireland.* Ithaca: Cornell University Press.

Bray, Dorothy. 1992. "A List of Motifs in the Lives of the Early Irish Saints." *Folklore Fellows Communications* CIX: 252.

Bynum, Caroline Walker. 1987. *Holy Feast and Holy Fast: The Religious Significance of Food to Medieval Women.* Berkeley: University of California Press.

Brown, Peter. 1982. *The Cult of the Saints: Its Rise and Function in Latin Christianity.* Chicago: University of Chicago Press.

Carmichael, Alexander. 1992. *Carmina Gadelica.* Edinburgh: Lindisfarne Press.

Coe, Paula Powers. 1988. *The Goddess Persistent: a Study of Traditions Surrounding Saint Brigit.* (Senior Thesis, unpublished).

Conolly, Sean. 1982. "Vita Prima Sanctae Brigitae: Background and Historical Value." *Journal of the Royal Society of Antiquaries of Ireland* 119: 5–49.

—and J.-M. Picard. 1987. "Cogitosus' Life of St. Brigit: Content and Value." *Journal of the Royal Society of Antiquaries of Ireland* 117: 5–27.

Danaher, Kevin. 1972. *The Year in Ireland.* Cork: The Mercier Press.

Ford, Patrick K. (trans.) 1977. *The Mabinogi and Other Welsh Tales.* Berkeley: University of California Press.

Glassie, Henry. 1982. *Passing the Time in Ballymenone: Culture and History of an Ulster Community.* Bloomington: Indiana University Press.

Kenney, James F. (1929) 1979. *The Sources for the Early History of Ireland: Ecclesiastical: An Introduction and Guide.* Dublin: Padraic O Tailliuir.

Lysaght, Patricia. 1994. "Women, Milk and Magic at the Boundary Feast of May." *In Milk and Milk Products from Medieval to Modern Times: Proceedings of the Ninth International Conference on Ethnological Food Research, Ireland, 1992*, edited by P. Lysaght. Edinburgh: Canongate Academic.

Macalister, R. A. S. 1919. "Temair Breg: A Study of the Remains and Traditions of Tara." *Proceedings of the Royal Irish Acadamy* XXIV.C, Nos. 10–11.

Mac Cana, Proinsias. 1970. *Celtic Mythology*. London: Hamlyn.

McNamara, Jo Ann, John E. Halborg, and E. Gordon Whatley. 1992. *Sainted Women of the Dark Ages*. Durham: Duke University Press.

O'Catháin, Séamas. 1995. *The Festival of Brigit: Celtic Goddess and Holy Woman*. Blackrock, County Dublin: DBA Publications.

O'hAodha, Donncha. 1978. *Bethu Brigte*. Dublin: Dublin Institute for Advanced Studies.

Patterson, J. Dean. 1982. "Kildare: The Cathedral Church of St. Brigid." Church of Ireland: Kildare.

Patterson, Nerys. 1994. Cattle Lords and Clansmen: The Social Structure of Early Ireland. Notre Dame: University of Notre Dame Press

Plummer, The Rev. Charles. (1910) 1968. *Vitae Sanctorum Hiberniae*. Oxford: Oxford University Press.

Quin, E. G. 1981. "The Early Irish Poem 'Isucán'." *Cambridge Medieval Celtic Studies* 1: 39–52.

Stokes, Whitley, ed. 1890. *Anecdota Oxoniensia: Lives of Saints from the Book of Lismore*. Oxford: Clarendon Press.

Reworking of
an 11th Century Irish Prayer to Brigit

Erin Johnson

Brigit,
Excellent, exalted one,
Bright, golden, quickening flame,
Shine your blessings upon us
from your eternal lands,
You, radiant fire of the sun.

BRIGIT: CAILLEACH AND MIDWIFE TO A NEW WORLD

Dolores Whelan

eflecting on the turmoil present in the world today, it is clear to all but those steeped in denial that all is not well. It seems that something ails us humans, something that causes us to live in ways that disrespect our mother—the living earth—and all our relatives. We ask what is it in us humans that creates such a restless world where there is little sense of belonging, nurture, or home, and that causes suffering to so many of the species with whom we share this planet?

The exclusion of the feminine energy in our naming and understanding of the divine is reflected in a corresponding absence and valuing of feminine energy in all aspects of life in western society. The devaluing and exclusion of feminine energy over the past centuries has created a distorted story about life that has resulted in a world whose shape and vibration creates disharmony.

So how do we find our way back to a more harmonious way of life? If we know what is missing and what ails us, it may be possible for us to make the journey back towards wholeness and health.

In times of great danger and challenges, cultures often seek the wisdom for the journey ahead in the stories and myths that sustained them in an earlier time. However, as poet Nuala Ni Dhomhnail suggests, this requires an understanding that "[a]ctual myths and stories themselves soar way above any uses to which they may have been put already and can and must be retranslated by each generation in terms of their own need and thus liberated into a new consciousness."

At the present time, there is a wonderful re-emergence of aspects of ancient spiritual traditions by people all over the world. The reconnection and embodiment of these ancient spiritual traditions, myths, and stories has the potential to release the spiritual power needed for us to become agents of transformation within our society.

At this time, many people are becoming aware of the wisdom of the feminine. Genuine feminine energy has been excluded from most institutions, both religious and secular, throughout western culture. To include the presence of the divine feminine energy in creating a world whose shape is more wholesome requires a fundamental reclaiming of the essential role of the feminine in all aspects of life. In order to create change within the physical world and in our society, it is necessary to change the dreams and stories held within the imagination of a society.

My own journey over the past 25 years has been primarily within the Celtic spiritual tradition. This tradition has emerged over many millennia and continues to evolve. It includes the wisdom of the megalithic, the pre-Christian Celtic, and the Christian Celtic traditions as they met and engaged with each other through the ages. I believe the rekindling of the flames of this tradition, which have lain dormant for many centuries, "like coals under the smooring awaiting a new kindling," holds a key to the recovery of the wisdom needed to create a more sane society.

"God is good and he has a great mother," a statement sometimes heard in Ireland, reflects an important truth at the heart of the Celtic spiritual tradition: honoring the presence of the divine feminine. The divine feminine, present at the heart of this spiritual tradition, plays a central role in both Celtic spirituality and Celtic culture. There are many goddesses within Celtic mythology; however, Brigit/Bridget, as both goddess and saint, occupies a central place as representative of the divine feminine in this tradition. Reconnecting with and re-membering the spirit and archetypal energy of Brigit, in both her goddess and saint manifestations, is an essential task of this renaissance. Brigit, although normally associated with the maiden and mother aspects of feminine energy, is also expressed in the *cailleach** form, as indicated in this prayer:

---

* Editor's Note: *Cailleach* has been defined as a divine hag, a creatix, ancestral deity or deified ancestor, the Celtic Goddess of Winter and the Land, Celtic Crone Goddess, and many more variations.

Molamid Brid an mhaighean;
Molamid Brid an mhathair;
Molamid Brid an cailleach.

Praise to Brigit the maiden;
Praise to Brigit, the mother;
Praise to Brigit, the crone

These three different but related manifestations together create a divine feminine trinity. Each aspect of this trinity occupies a different role on the life, death, and rebirth continuum. The feminine energy is both the harbinger and the birther of new life and is the destroyer of life that has been spent. It is experienced at the thresholds of life and death, death and rebirth.

In the past two decades, there has been a new awakening of the importance of Brigit and her place within our lives and our world. Her feast day at Imbolc is now celebrated in many places in Ireland and all over the world. There is an understanding that what is needed now is for people, individually and collectively, to recover those qualities that Brigit embodied in her lifetime, marking her as a woman of true spiritual power.

As we consider Saint Bridget, as reflected in the stories of her life as abbess of Kildare, Ireland, it is obvious that these qualities are similar to those present in her incarnation as the pre-Christian goddess. Bridget is considered a threshold person, one who can straddle both sides and remain detached. This quality, which is central in her life, is highlighted in the stories of her birth, which attest that she was born on the threshold of the house, neither within nor without; that her father was a noble man and her mother a slave; and that her father was a pagan and her mother a Christian. From Bridget's origins, she has this ability to stand in the void and remain centered within it, while holding the creative tension between two opposite perspectives. Many stories from her life portray her as a person capable of resolving conflicts in a healthy manner. Being centered and aligned within herself, she is detached and can grasp the energies of both sides clearly, thereby facilitating resolution. She has the ability to stand still and remain focused, in spite of the uncertainty present in the outer world.

As a child and a young woman, Bridget constantly challenged the accepted norms of her society, especially those expressed by her father when they opposed her own values. This shows Bridget as a person who lived her life from a place of deep inner knowing and inner authority. She also refused to marry any of the suitors that her father arranged for her because she had chosen a different life path and destiny; she would not compromise her soul journey.

Bridget's legendary generosity appears in numerous stories of her giving away food and clothes to people who came to her monastery or whom she met along the way. This generosity was, it seems, based on her absolute faith in the abundance of the universe to provide all that was needed in each moment. Each time she gave away the butter or meat needed for the next meal, it miraculously reappeared in time for that meal.

Bridget's capacity to bring forth new life, to nourish, to create plenty in the crops or an abundance of the milk from cows, and to manifest or create *ex nihilo* (out of nothing) is a reflection of the true abundance and the prosperity of the society, living in relationship with the land, created by her. Her life and work thrived because of her deep trust and absence of fear.

It is said that from the moment Bridget learned to know God, her mind remained ever focused on God. She remained connected to God and the heavens while living on the earthly plane. Her power of manifestation was a result of this ability to be aligned with heaven and earth. The strong connection between her inner and outer worlds allowed her to focus her energy onto a particular intention and ensure its manifestation.

The story of how Bridget got the land for her monastery in Kildare is a wonderful example of her ability to manifest what is needed. She stated clearly what she needed and asked the local lord for land. First, he refused, but she was not deterred. She pursued her request in a different way by asking, "Give me what land my mantle will cover," to which he said yes. When she placed the mantle on the ground, it grew until it covered enough land for the monastery. This story reflects a woman who can hold her intention clearly, even when on the surface it seems that her request will not be met.

These inspiring stories of Bridget relate to her active life in the world, where she embodies and lives true spiritual power. But what and where is the source of this power? To fully understand the power and the qualities that Bridget embodied, as reflected in the many stories about her life, we need to begin with an exploration of the role of Bridget as *cailleach*, the aspect of the divine feminine that rules during the season of Samhain (winter) at the beginning of the Celtic year. This, I believe, is the wellspring from which Bridget's power manifests in the world.

What, then, is the energy associated with the hag, crone, or *cailleach* aspect of the divine feminine? The *cailleach* is the embodiment of the tough mother-love that challenges her children to stop acting in destructive ways. It is the energy that refuses to indulge in inappropriate personal or societal dreams. It is the energy that will bring death to those dreams and fantasies that are not aligned with our highest good. Yet, this *cailleach* energy also will support the emergence and manifestation in the world of the highest and deepest within us. It will hold us safely as we embrace the darkness within ourselves and our society. It is an energy that insists that we stand still, open our hearts, and feel our own pain and the pain of the earth. This is the energy that teaches us how to stay with the process when things are difficult. This energy will not allow us to run away.

The *cailleach's* way of being is a slow, inwardly focused way, with minimum outward activity—a way that values times of active waiting, waiting that pays attention and allows life to unfold.

An essential part of the journey that all the great heroes and heroines in world mythologies undertake includes facing and embracing the energy of surrender, darkness, and death. The hero or heroine learns the next step required in their outer world journey only by submitting to and being initiated into the dark world of the *cailleach*. Through this initiation, the mature masculine power can emerge and lead each person to find their true path. When this happens, the action that follows will be in the service of the true feminine and bring forth wisdom and compassion, creating new life, vitality, and sustainability. However, because western society is currently dominated by the young masculine energy present in both men and women, characterized by its "can do" attitude, there is an urgent need for each of us to make this heroic journey with the *cailleach*, so that we will become agents for the transformation of our society.

A story from the Celtic tradition illustrates the importance of the *cailleach* and her energy. Niall of the Nine Hostages and his four brothers come to a well to get a drink of water. The well was being guarded by an old woman (who represents the *cailleach* or hag). When the first brother went to the well, she told him that, if he wanted to drink the water, he must give her a kiss; he was horrified and refused, so she sent him away. The other three brothers went in turn on the same errand, and each refused to kiss the hag. As the story goes, in Jan de Fouw's translation:

> Then it was Niall's turn. Faced with the same challenge, he kissed the old hag and embraced her. When he looked again, she had changed into the most beautiful woman in the world. "What art thou?" said the boy. "King of Tara, I am Sovereignty . . . your seed shall be over every clan."

This story suggests that, in order to have access to the life-enhancing energy represented by the water in the well, it is necessary for the young masculine to embrace this particular, and perhaps unattractive, aspect of the feminine energy. Why is this so? The *cailleach* represents the wisdom gathered by living in right relationship with the earth, something that requires reflection, stillness, and attentiveness. It knows more clearly what is needed and what is possible in each situation, and it is aware of the consequences of particular actions. It knows how to proceed slowly; it understands the value of times of waiting and times of allowing. It knows how to be and how to act.

So how can we—you and I—begin the journey back towards wholeness and balance?

Brigit, in her *cailleach* form, can help us to embrace these difficult and fearful aspects of our lives. The cauldron, a central image in the Celtic and other traditions, is a vessel for transformation and transmutation. In many stories, the cauldron is first filled with unpalatable raw things, which then are used to create a nourishing soup using the transforming energy of the universe through the action of fire and water. The transformation of the contents of the cauldron is supervised by the *cailleach* energy, which works inwardly, quietly, and slowly to bring about an unforced and timely rebirth. The transformation of the cauldron's contents concentrates their essence and offers them back in a new and more suitable form. From this process, we learn that the possibility of transformation and rebirth always exists, no matter how devitalized something appears to be. A new rebirth can be achieved when we submit ourselves and our concerns to the inward and slow transformational energy of the cauldron and the *cailleach*.

Philosopher Richard Kearney, in his poem "Brigit's Well," speaks of the importance of this inward and downward journey and suggests that it is the only way to access the life-giving and inspiring fire of Brigit that lies underneath the water.

I will rest now at the bottom of Brigit's well
I will follow the crow's way
Footprint by footprint
In the mud down here
I won't come up
Until I am calmed down
And the earth dries beneath me
And I have paced the caked ground
Until smooth all over
It can echo a deeper voice
Mirror a longer shadow

This poem suggests the importance of that deep journey to the well where the source of new life and the fire of passion is found. At Imbolc, Brigit appears as the fresh maiden of springtime emerging from the womb of the *cailleach*, Queen of Winter. The tiny spark of new light discovered in the deep, womb-darkness of the winter solstice has grown sufficiently to safely emerge from that inner world and begins its transformation of winter into spring. Now Brigit embodies the energy that breathes life into

117

the mouth of dead winter. The energy of Brigit at Imbolc is the energy of "yes". It can only emerge from the place of stillness.

Brigit is also closely associated with the life-giving aspect of fire, a fire that doesn't burn but which can never be fully quenched. When this fire comes from a clear and deep space, as happens following the inward journey, it will be significant and filled with truth and potency. This life-giving fire will act within individuals, within the land, in the relationships between the people and their land, fanning the fires of creative endeavor so that all forms of life can partake in the symphony of new life emerging each springtime. Richard Kearney also speaks of the re-emergence of a new fire born of a deeper place within:

> Then the fire may come again
> Beneath me, this time
> Rising beyond me
>
> No narcissus-flinted spark
> Behind closed eyes
> But a burning bush
>
> A fire that always burns away
> But never is burnt out

The fire discovered through this deep journey is an inner light that guides each of us to find our next step.

I believe that the archetypal energy of Brigit, the embodiment of the divine feminine present within the Celtic tradition, has the capacity to lead and support us in transforming the present wasteland into a new life-sustaining society. For this to happen, we need to understand that the archetypal energy that Brigit represents is a real aspect of the human psyche, one that has been largely dormant over the past few hundred years but is now re-emerging. Each of us can become keeper of the Brigit flame by developing and living those qualities and values that distinguished her. As we align ourselves with her archetypal energies, she supports us to courageously and safely face the demons of this time. She teaches us how to stand still in a wobbling world, to act as a unifying force, to hold the space of possibility, and so become agents of transformation.

So we ask that, in the words of the commonly-known prayer:

The mantle of Brigit about us
The memory of Brigit within us
The protection of Brigit keeping us from harm,
from ignorance, from heartlessness this day from dawn till dark.

When we embrace her energy, Brigit will hold us and guide us through this transition. I believe she is the one who has the power to awaken in each of us what the traditional Celtic triad calls, "an eye to see what is, the heart that feels what is, and the courage that dares to follow."

REFERENCES:

ni Dhomhnail, Nuala. 2000. "Afterword" In *Amergin* by Jan de Fouw. Dublin: Wolfhound Press.

Kearney, Richard. 2001. "Brigit's Well." In *The Irish Soul* in Dialogue by Stephen J. Collins. Dublin: The Liffey Press.

Dawn at Bridget's Well

Patricia Monaghan

In hope, in pain, in song we passed the night.
We have kept watch—kept faith—each in our way.
Our long dark vigil ends in spring's mild light.

We ended winter with this ancient rite,
Strangers until we joined our hands to pray.
In hope, in pain, in song we passed the night.

Beside the guttering candles, a single white
Snowdrop nods to greet St. Bridget's day.
A long dark vigil ends in spring's mild light.

So much is wrong, across the world: we fight
Each other, blight the land, betray
Our hopes. In plaintive song we passed the night.

Yet we believe and pray, acolytes
In service to a change too long delayed.
Our long dark vigil ends in spring's mild light

And we rise, renewed. Such ritual ignites
The fire in our souls. It's a new day.
In hope, in pain, in song we passed the night.
The long dark vigil ends in spring's mild light.

THE FEAST DAY OF SAINT BRIDGET AND OTHER STORIES

Carol P. Christ

The Christian feast day of Saint Bridget of Kildare, one of the two patron saints of Ireland, is held on February 1, the pre-Christian holiday known as Imbolc. Imbolc marked the day that cows and ewes gave birth and began to produce milk. Marija Gimbutas says it was also the day when hibernating snakes (like North American groundhogs) first emerged from their holes. In northern European countries, Imbolc signals the beginning of the end of winter. The days begin to lengthen perceptibly after the winter solstice, but the sun appears to stand still, and it seems that winter will never end.

At Imbolc, spring is not yet in full blossom, but if hibernating snakes come out of their holes, it is a sure sign that the processes of transformation will continue and warmer days will not be far off. As Gimbutas says, "The awakening of the snakes meant the awakening of all of nature, the beginning of the life of the new year." Saint Bridget's male counterpart, Saint Patrick, was said to have driven all of the snakes out of Ireland, a legend that reiterates the Biblical association of snakes with evil and temptation. Yet in Old Europe, snakes were positively valued: snakes were symbolically associated with life and regeneration. Moreover, snakes eat mice and rats, protecting granaries and helping to create hygiene and, therefore, health in the home. In driving snakes out of Ireland, Saint Patrick—like his precursors, Marduk, Apollo, and Saint George—was re-enacting the myth of slaying the goddess or her sacred companion. Saint Patrick may not have driven all of the snakes out of Ireland, but Christianity succeeded in making fear and hatred of snakes nearly universal in Christian cultures. Yet in the Lithuania of Gimbutas' youth, protective snakes were encouraged to live underneath houses and were fed with bowls of milk. Could it be that, in some countries, snakes were lured out of their holes at Imbolc by the setting-out of bowls of the first milk produced by the lactating ewes and cows? I find this is likely. However, it seems that there never were snakes in Ireland.

For agricultural peoples, the day that cows and ewes give birth is not simply another marker of the coming of spring. When human beings domesticated cattle and sheep by providing them with food, care, and shelter, we began to depend upon these animals for milk, cheese, butter, yogurt, meat, leather, and wool. In domesticated herds and flocks, most of the animals are female because the females give birth and produce milk. A few of the males will be allowed to survive, but most will be eaten on feast days and at celebrations of birth and marriage. Agricultural peoples knew that males were needed to impregnate the females, but in celebrating the day that ewes and cows gave birth and began to produce milk, our Old European ancestors were affirming female power to give birth and nurture life. For them, Imbolc was a reminder that the lives of human beings and animals are intertwined in the processes of birth, death, and regeneration in the web of life, which they understood to be the cycles of the body of the goddess.

As long as agricultural peoples continued in their traditional ways, this embodied knowing was never fully lost. As Gimbutas tells us:

> The Old European sacred images and symbols were never totally uprooted; these most persistent features in human history were too deeply implanted in the psyche . . . Some of the old traditions, particularly those connected with birth, death, and earth fertility rituals, have continued to this day without much change in some regions; in others they were assimilated into Indo-European ideology.

The stories told about Saint Bridget confirm this. Not only was her feast day set on Imbolc, but also the legends of Saint Bridget connect her to the nourishment provided by the milk of ewes and cows. The Abbess

Bridget's cows miraculously gave milk three times in one day, creating a veritable lake of milk. Milk was poured on the ground on Saint Bridget's day. At Bridget's shrine in County Louth at Faughart, on July 12, 1986, six young girls were seen dressed in white, the color of milk.

Saint Bridget has the same name as the pre-Christian goddess of Ireland. According to Miranda Green, the name Brigit is from the Celtic *brig*, meaning "high one" or "exalted one." This suggests that Brigit was understood to be a mountain mother whose body rose in the landscape. In the times of Roman occupation, Brigit was identified with Minerva. Both goddesses were associated with healing, with the arts of spinning and weaving, and with the blacksmith's craft. According to Miranda Green, "little is known in detail about the goddess Brigit." She cautions against assuming that the legends of Saint Bridget can help us to re-member the goddess.

The methods of Gimbutas suggest otherwise. In a very important sense, the goddess never died. She lived on wherever people continued to remember her. Priests and theologians may have said that Saint Bridget was not a goddess, but many people—especially women who needed a divinity who understood their lives and problems—honored Saint Bridget as if she were the goddess Brigit. Gimbutas suggests that, when the goddess could not be worshipped overtly, she

> . . . gradually retreated into the depths of the forests or onto mountaintops, where she remains to this day in beliefs and fairy stories . . . In some nooks of Europe . . . there still flow sacred and miraculous rivers and springs, there flourish holy forests and groves, reservoirs of blossoming life, there grow gnarled trees blossoming with vitality and holding the power to heal; along waters there still stand menhirs, called 'Goddesses,' full of mysterious power.

Those of us whose ancestors came to North America from elsewhere are no longer connected to places in natural landscapes venerated from time immemorial, encoding our ancentors' embodied and embedded knowing of the sacredness of nature and our connection to its powers. Yet even we sometimes sense the sacred in the natural beauty of the American land.

Everyone who visits the ancient shrine of a saint in Europe will encounter the Old European goddess in sacred places in nature that have been rededicated to a Christian saint. In County Kildare in Ireland, Saint Bridget's major shrine is associated with oak groves, a river and a sacred well, and a group of stones, including a large black rock. A sacred tree or grove, holy water, and a sacred rock or stone—these are exactly the places in nature that Gimbutas designated as the "retreats" of the goddess.

Audrey Whitson tells us that pilgrims approach Saint Bridget's shrine by following a country lane "lined in oak trees, trunks two feet broad, sleeved in ivy, thick and gnarled, one hundred, two hundred years old." The life of a tree is longer than that of a woman or a man; a tree's times of fullness and bounty, as well as its cycles of renewal after death in winter, have long been viewed as source and symbol of the powers of birth, death, and regeneration. For these and other reasons, our Old European ancestors felt sacred power in trees and worshipped in groves.

"When you enter the well site at Kildare, you cross over a bridge and under a trellis, a threshold of water and willow," Whitson says. At the approach to the well, "streams from the well are channeled through two huge carved rocks, holes where nipples might be. The Irish call these the Paps of Brighid." The well itself is surrounded by "[r]ound, smooth slate slabs" with stone steps leading down to its inner chamber, a kind of womb. Healing and life-giving water was associated with the nurturing powers of the goddess in Old Europe. Between the well and its channels, stands a shrine with a black, basalt base, which Whitson describes as possibly "the oldest thing in the whole shrine." It has been touched and rubbed smooth by many hands. Near this are five "chair stones." In Old Europe, black is the color of fertile and transforming earth, and black stones were often understood to be aniconic appearances of the goddess.

By visiting the shrine of Saint Bridget in the flesh, we gain the embodied, embedded knowing of her connection to the powers of birth, death, and regeneration in the earth and the body of the goddess. Failing an actual visit, we can visit her shrine in our imaginations, connecting stories of Saint Bridget with our own intuitions of the sacredness of the natural world. We can find oak groves, springs, and black stones in our own landscapes, recreating shrines and places of worship and pilgrimage that re-imagine the human connection to the natural world. If cows and ewes are not symbols but living creatures sacred to Saint Bridget and Brigit, can we re member her yet countenance factory farming? "Human alienation from the vital roots of earthly life," may be part of our heritage, Gimbutas tells us; but, she says, "the cycles never stop turning, and now we find the Goddess reemerging from the forests and mountains, bringing us hope for the future, returning us to our most ancient human roots."

In this story, I describe a ritual I created for Brigid's Place, which I enacted with others at Christ Church Cathedral in Houston, Texas. It suggests one way we can connect with Saint Bridget and with Brigit, no matter where we are.

Before the ritual began, we set two altars and a potted tree in place. The first altar was the shrine of the Black Stone, which in this case was a stone that had previously been used in dream workshops at Brigid's Place. This altar was draped with a white cloth and, beside the stone, it held a vase of opening roses, a triangular-shaped stone image of Saint Bridget, a bowl of milk, two chalices filled with milk, and five votive candles. The second altar, the shrine of the Holy Well, was draped with Irish lace, and in its center was a beautiful footed silver punch bowl filled with water and surrounded by votive candles. Women from the workshop placed their personal offerings on this altar. A basket with ribbons was placed next to the potted tree, representing the Sacred Tree of Life, symbol of Saint Bridget and Brigit.

Before the ritual began, the women lined up in crone-ological order, oldest to youngest. The eldest was asked to be the "guide" at the shrine of the Black Stone, the youngest at the Sacred Tree, and the one exactly in the middle at the Holy Well. They took their places at the shrines. The others formed a line that became a large circle as the "pilgrims" passed by the shrines.

The ritual leader said, "Think of yourself as a pilgrim to the shrine of Saint Bridget in Kildare. As you wait in line, meditate on why you have come here, what you hope will be healed or transformed in you, what you have to offer."

At the shrine of the Black Stone, the crone, who was seated, handed the Black Stone to each pilgrim in turn, saying, "Hold the Black Stone, symbol of Saint Bridget and Brigit. Let your energy mingle with hers." Although this was not part of the plan, the crone spoke so loudly that her voice was heard by all the pilgrims throughout the ritual, the words she spoke becoming a kind of mantra that kept us focused.

At the shrine of the Holy Well, the woman in the fullness of life directed the pilgrims, saying, "Gaze into the healing Holy Water, symbol of Saint Bridget and Brigit. Let yourself be healed."

At the Sacred Tree, the maiden offered each pilgrim a ribbon, saying, "Look upon the Tree of Life, symbol of Saint Bridget and Brigit. With your ribbon, offer your gifts."

When the last pilgrim had tied her ribbon to the tree, the women joined hands in a circle, and sang:

As we bless the Source of Life,
So we are blessed.*

The chalices of milk were offered to the pilgrims, with words repeated slowly several times by the ritual leader as the chalices around the circle: "This is the day that the cows and the ewes give birth. Taste this milk, given to you."

When all had tasted the milk, the pilgrims sang again:

As we bless the Source of Life,
So we are blessed.

---

* Author's Note: The song, "As We Bless the Source of Life," is by Faith Rogow.

The leader closed the ritual: "May we venerate Saint Bridget in the fullness of her connection to bountiful and life-giving earth, the Goddess Brigit, in whom we live and move and have our being."

On my first visit to Ireland, I had the opportunity to visit Bridget's Well on Faughart Hill with Irish mythologist and former Green Party European Parliamentarian Nuala Ahern, and my friend, feminist scholar Naomi Goldenberg. Nuala picked us up in Dublin and we drove north for about an hour. Our first stop was at the Roman Catholic shrine near a stream and a wood where Saint Bridget was said to have worked as a child. Signs prohibited leaving personal offerings, but someone had ignored them and placed candles around the modern sculpture.

Nuala took us on to the well on Faughart Hill, which she considered more sacred. She told us it is visited on February 1, and added that her grandmother often brought her there when she was a child. I recalled the special times in early mornings when my Irish grandmother brought me with her to church in San Francisco, where she lit candles and said the rosary in the quiet darkness. The well is covered by a beehive structure and I, being tall, had to crouch to enter it. Next to the well, pilgrims had left offerings—bits of cloth, photographs, key rings, and even cigarette lighters on a tree and in a wicker basket set in front of it.

Nuala had just put a deposit on a new home. Standing in front of the well she asked Bridget—saint and goddess—to bless her move and to make her new home as happy as her last one had been. Naomi asked to be able to let go of her worries about her grown daughter. I asked for the burden of despair I was carrying about the destruction of the environment in Lesbos to be lifted so that I could enjoy life and work to preserve what is left. We drank from the waters of the well, and then giddily sprinkled them all over each other. None of us had brought anything to leave on the tree, so Nuala suggested that we leave our lipsticks ("What could be more personal than that?") in the basket. Then we followed her in the Irish tradition of walking three times around the well in the direction of the sun's movement. While we walked in the damp grass, a verse from a familiar song came into my body: "This is my mother's world and to my listening ears, all nature sings and 'round me rings the music of the spheres." I sang it out loud.

I don't know if Nuala's and Naomi's prayers were answered, but mine was. When I got home, I took up a suggestion made by Nuala that I write an official Complaint to the European Commission detailing the failure to protect bird and wildlife habitats on Lesbos under the Natura 2000 law. What seemed like a week's project grew like topsy as I gathered the hundreds of letters to and from the Greek government, all concerning degradation of wetlands, into a massive Complaint to the European Commission. The Complaint took the better part of the year to write but, after a long process involving difficult negotiations and two rewritings, it was eventually signed by the World Wildlife Fund – Greece, as well as the Hellenic Ornithological Society. It is currently under serious consideration by the European Commission. I suspect Nuala also passed the Green Party torch on to me at Bridget's Well, for I have now been asked to run as a candidate for the Green Party in three separate elections in Lesbos.

I had a kind of mystical experience of Irish women's rituals when Naomi and I were left alone in the shadowy depths of the basement of the National Museum of Dublin with *sheela-na-gigs** collected from various places in Ireland. *Sheela-na-gigs* are carved images of naked women, many of whom seem to be old women, who display their vulvas. Two are on display in the museum, and the rest are kept below ground. Sheelas were often placed in churches, and a popular interpretation is that they were a warning against lust, the sin of Eve. However, the *sheelas'* origins are likely to be pre-Christian. As Naomi and I looked closely at

---

*Author's Note: Photographs of the *sheela-na-gigs* can be found on www.irelands-sheelanagigs.org.

the images in the museum, I suddenly noticed that some of the *sheelas* seemed to be dancing. The Burgesbeg *sheela* seemed to me to be leaping or jumping (her toes are pointed and her feet do not touch the ground), while the Ballylarkin *sheela* (whose pose is usually described as "sitting on her hunkers") seemed to be about to spring up into the leap of the Burgesbeg *sheela*, or to have just landed.

As my vision continued, I saw old women on dark nights at holy wells, sacred trees, and graveyards. Everywhere, they were joyously leaping and jumping while displaying their vulvas. They were warning the Christians, "Don't forget the mother." Some might have viewed such women as frightening, disgusting, or mad. But those who had not forgotten the mother, I imagined, would have smiled and given the old women a wink. Was my vision far-fetched? Barbara Freitag cites an early 20th century report of a ritual dance at a holy well. "The women, with garments fastened right up under their arms and with hands joined, were dancing in a circle round the well. An aged crone sat in their midst, and dipping a small vessel in the water, kept sprinkling them. They were married women who had proved childless and had come to the well to experience its fertilizing virtues." Though she does not recognize *sheelas* as dancing, Freitag connects "gig" to "jig" and "gigue"—folk dances requiring fast footwork.

I find it likely that priests removed *sheelas* from pagan holy places and set them in rural churches, often above doors, to lure the women into the church, and as warnings against rituals they hoped to eradicate. To the priests, the *sheelas* may have symbolized the sin of Eve. But the Irish love a good joke. I like to think of the people crossing themselves as they walked under the *sheelas* and silently affirming, "We do not forget the mother."

REFERENCES:

Christ, Carol P. 1998. *Rebirth of the Goddess*. New York: Routledge.

Gimbutas, Marija. 2001. *The Language of the Goddess*. London: Thames & Hudson.

Green, Miranda. 1996. *Celtic Goddesses*. New York: G. Braziller.

Frietag, Barbara. 2004. *Sheela-Na-Gig: Unravelling an Enigma*. London: Routledge.

Whitson, Audrey J. 2003. "Meditations." *Journal of Feminist Studies* in Religion 19/1: 71–75.

BRIGIT
IN THE TWENTY-FIRST CENTURY

A Garden for Brigit

Jenny Beale

In 2004, we opened Brigit's Garden in County Galway on the west coast of Ireland as a place where people could engage with nature and the Brigit tradition in beautiful and tranquil surroundings. The gardens are a unique blend of Celtic wisdom and contemporary design, sculpting and arranging the elements of the local landscape—water, stone, earth, wood, and plants—to create spaces that are richly symbolic. The heart of the project is four gardens representing the old Celtic seasonal festivals, so a walk through the gardens is a journey through the cycle of the year and the cycle of life.

Brigit is a historical figure, so why name a garden after her in the 21st century? From early European beginnings to the Celtic goddess of the land, and from early Christian saint to modern icon, the interpretation of Brigit has changed and adapted to the needs of each generation, yet the tradition has always carried a core of deeply rooted symbolism and teachings. There is great wisdom in the Brigit tradition, which can inspire and guide us today as we seek to weave new patterns of meaning. In this short article, I will outline some relevant aspects of the Brigit tradition and how we respond to them in Brigit's Garden.

The first of these is the association of Brigit and nature. In the modern world, we are taught a linear view of time: past, present, and future are seen as a straight line, with a strong sense of forward movement and a drive for "progress." The Celtic year was different. It was seen as a circle, a cycle, divided into four quarters of three months each. The yearly cycle mirrored the cycle of life. As the old year died at Samhain (Hallowe'en), the new year began; out of death came rebirth, and out of darkness, light.

135

The Celtic day began at dusk and the Celtic year began at the start of the darkest months, reflecting an understanding that birth, growth, and new beginnings need to be nurtured in the darkness, and that the dark is a place of creativity, not of fear. After gestation in the winter came birth and youth in the spring, starting with the celebration of Brigit's Day on February 1. Summer, beginning at Bealtaine in May, was considered the time for lovers, marriages, and young adulthood. Lughnasa, in August, marked the harvest and autumn quarter, when life moved into fullness, maturity, and old age. In Brigit's Garden, each festival is represented by a garden designed to reflect the qualities of each season.

Paying attention to the seasons and what they represent can help us feel grounded, to remember that we are a part of nature, not separate from it, and to get many insights into the rhythms of our lives. As well as representing the full life cycle, the seasonal changes can symbolize a phase within life, or any project or piece of work that begins with an idea, grows, and is born, develops, matures, and wanes.

Brigit was also closely associated with the wisdom in nature. Celtic culture held certain trees in high regard: hazel was the tree of wisdom, hawthorn the fairy tree, and oak the tree of strength and kingship. Brigit's monastery was in Kildare, *Cill Dara*, or "the Church of the Oak Grove." Celtic mythology abounds with stories of shamanic shape-shifting involving salmon, eagles, hawks, and other creatures, stories that taught about reverence for nature and the benefits of learning about, and learning from, the local flora and fauna.

One of the best known stories of Bridget concerns her magical cloak. The young Saint Bridget went to the local king to ask for land for her monastery. The king told her he would only give her as much land as her cloak would cover. So she laid her cloak on the ground and it spread and spread, covering a huge area of good land around Kildare that ensured food and wealth for her monastery. This story can be read in many ways; one interpretation is that the cloak symbolizes protection for the land it covers, acknowledging humans' dependence on the land for food and well-being, and the need to look after it sustainably.

The tradition of making Brigit's crosses was also strongly rooted in the land. The crosses were not made from precious metals and displayed in churches, but woven from the humblest plant growing locally in damp fields, the common rush. The rushes were picked on Brigit's Eve or on Brigit's Day and woven by family and friends around the fireside. The simple plant took on a sacred purpose, and the crosses were hung over the doorway as a blessing and protection for the household.

The second aspect of the Brigit tradition that we pay attention to at Brigit's Garden is her connection with the divine feminine. It is no accident that the feast day chosen for Bridget, the early Celtic Christian saint, was February 1, the date of the old spring festival of Imbolc. Many stories and symbols from the pre-Christian goddess Brigit became associated with Saint Bridget, bringing many aspects of the Celtic relationship with the land into Christian times. Brigit was said to breathe life into dead winter, her warm breath waking up the land again. In early February, the snowdrops bloom and the first lambs are born; the year has turned, the sun is strengthening, and life returns once more. The association with spring and milk links Brigit to earlier fertility goddesses. She was also the patron of midwives and healers, and as midwife she birthed many kinds of new life in the spring. Brigit carried the thread of the divine feminine that wove through history and celebrated women's powers of fertility, childbirth, and nurturing. The Brigit tradition can still help women feel empowered and can enable both women and men to celebrate the feminine side of their natures.

The third aspect is the connection between Brigit and community. Another interpretation of the story of Brigit's cloak is that it represented protection and community. The cloak connected all those within it, bringing them under her care and protection and building a community. According to one story, Saint Bridget continued to look after her religious community after her death. There were nineteen nuns who took turns in tending the sacred fire, which was never allowed to go out. On the twentieth day, they left the fire for Bridget to tend; even though she was no longer alive, the fire burned bright and left no ashes.

Brigit has always been important to rural people for the health and well-being of their families, their animals, and the land. Many Brigit traditions were, and are still, family- and village-based—essentially domestic practices taking place around the hearth, which is the heart of the house. There is an equality and sense of sharing in these traditions and in the absence of the hierarchies found in the organized Church.

In Brigit's Garden, we reflect many of these rich threads in the design of the gardens themselves, and in the activities that take place within them. The symbolism in the four seasonal gardens is there for those who seek it, though the gardens can be enjoyed without necessarily engaging with the Celtic themes. The intention is to provide a unique and beautiful place where people can relax and appreciate nature in their own way. There is fun, too, and the woodlands, ponds, and meadows provide magical places for children to explore. There are many primary-school visits, and the children get an opportunity to get hands-on with nature and make connections with their Celtic heritage.

We are developing creative, contemporary ways of celebrating the seasonal festivals, whether it is welcoming people to a community bonfire for the summer solstice, spooky story-telling at Hallowe'en, or making crosses on Brigit's Day. We also welcome groups with an interest in Brigit from many different countries.

In a world where the loss of connection between humankind and nature is endangering our futures in so many ways, we need to rediscover our sacred relationship with the natural world. To do this, I believe we have to engage people's hearts and spirits, not just their minds. The Brigit tradition can open our eyes to the rich tapestry that weaves together people, the land, story, spirit and nature, and inspires us to live more authentic and balanced lives. My hope is that Brigit's Garden will play its own small part in this process.

Bealtaine

The processional way between standing stones in the Bealtaine (summer) garden. *Photo by Joe O'Shaughnessy.*

Lughnasa

Stone circles for dancing and feasting in the Lughnasa (harvest and autumn) garden. *Photo by Airshots.*

The Autumn Apples
Celebrating abundance with autumn apples.
Photo by Martina Regan.

The Roundhouse
The thatched Roundhouse is a special place for meditation and gatherings. *Photo by Sabina Monaghan.*

MY BLOOD SONG

Szmeralda Shanel

"You were mine many times before now." The goddess Brigit calls to me.

"My flames will transform you, my waters will heal you." The goddess Brigit calls to me.

But I am a priestess of the dark mother Auset, a daughter of Sothis.

"You are my daughter too." The goddess Brigit calls to me.

But I am a priestess of the dark mother Auset, a daughter of Serpent.

"I am the Serpent too." The goddess Brigit calls to me.

But I am a priestess of the sight and sacred arts.

"I am the fiery arrow, the illuminating light of foresight, the spark that ignites and inspires creativity." The goddess Brigit calls to me.

But I am a priestess who honors my ancestors.

"I am your ancestor." The goddess Brigit calls to me.

I am an African American priestess primarily serving deities of Africa and the Diaspora. In the traditions of Africa and the Diaspora, ancestor reverence is of utmost importance. As a black person in

America, living with the legacy of slavery and all that it entails, it has been difficult for me to honor my European ancestors. How do I honor ancestors who most likely became ancestors by raping my other ancestors? How do I, as a priestess, honor certain ancestors, while ignoring others who are also responsible for my existence?

This is the problem with being spiritual. One moment, you're minding your own business, walking the path in beauty, wisdom, and all that good stuff. The next moment, without clear warning, you find you are being stalked by your own shadow: it's lurking here and there, haunting you, challenging you to look at what you thought you were beyond, or at least already doing right. Don't get me wrong. I am not one who is afraid of the dark. I am a priestess of Black Isis. But when it came to facing the truth of who I am biologically and how it connects to my spiritual work and experience, things got very uncomfortable.

When I traced my ancestry back through slavery on plantations in the American south, one thing was quite clear: my family's recorded history shows time and time again children born to enslaved black women and white men. Some of these men owned my ancestresses as slaves; while others may not have owned them, they certainly were in positions that gave them the power to do as they wished with them, without any consequence.

There are folks in my family who like to tell stories about possible affairs between slave and master. I am a romantic for sure, but I don't buy bullshit: a slave is property and property cannot give consent. For this reason, I am more inclined to believe what I know to be historically true: slave masters, overseers, and other white men who had access, systematically raped slaves.

I am tormented by the fact that I can trace my European ancestry back to specific countries, and these ancestors have names that I know and remember. My African ancestors were enslaved and given the names of the ones who owned them. Their true names and countries of origin are lost to me. And here I stand, blood pulsing through me, DNA spiraling, humming ancient tunes from various Celtic lands. These strange soul songs, a subtle ache winding between and wrapping around the strong polyrhythmic drum songs of Mother Africa and the chant songs of the indigenous people of the American southeast. My ancestral song haunts me.

I am not ashamed of this music, but neither am I exactly proud. It is true that perhaps these white men were not *all* rapists, but the fact still remains that many of them were. Now how do I honor all parts of my blood song?

I am stalked by my shadow, especially when the dark time of the year approaches and I start planning a feasting party for the ancestors. By candlelight, we sit in circle, me and my sista priestesses (other black women who serve the goddess and the ancestors). The conversation goes like this:

"What should we do about the other ones? Should we feed them too?"

"If we do, they can't be on the same altar as our Black and Native American ancestors."

"Maybe we should just feed the women."

"Why? They owned slaves, too, and looked the other way when their husbands, brothers, and sons raped our great-great-great grandmothers."

"Damn . . . It gets real when you say it like that . . . our great-great-great grandmothers . . . "

"What about further back? You know the ancestors of those ancestors, the ones who had nothing to do with slavery?"

"Fine, tonight we will feed them—but on a separate altar."

Six years ago was the first Hallowe'en/Samhain I even considered acknowledging my ancestors from the British Isles. At first, it was in small, synchronistic ways in my day-to-day, mundane experience that the goddess Brigit started to make herself present in my life. I would stumble across an article online or I would hear a snippet of a conversation where someone would mention Brigit, the goddess or the saint. There were times in early February, the time of her yearly celebration of Imbolc, that I would *feel* her energy in my home near my altar. On a few occasions, I was even asked to invoke her in public Imbolc rituals. This was all fine and good. I honor and respect all goddesses and was always happy to welcome and celebrate Brigit in ritual with others. Still, I had no personal interest in committing to do any deep personal work with her.

Eventually, she started to show up in very potent ways. I was looking for a teacher in the Anderson Faery/Feri tradition. I had always been interested and intrigued by Feri because, while it is a tradition with many Celtic influences and aspects, it is an American witchcraft tradition with roots in Africa and incorporates African and African Diasporic elements in the teachings and practices. The day I contacted the woman who would become my teacher and initiator, she said, "Oh, wow! I've been working with Brigit, and I was *just* at my altar telling her I needed another female student—and then you called."

Sometime later, I spent a weekend at a goddess temple where I was leading a ceremony. At night and in the early morning, the space was closed to visitors, and I had the temple to myself. One night, when I stood in the back of the temple before my mother Isis/Auset's altar to commune with her, she sent me to the front of the temple, to Brigit's Well. Why, I did not know, but I followed her instructions. I sat before Brigit's Well, said a simple prayer, and tossed coins into the waters. Suddenly, something loosened inside of me, a powerful force rushed through me, and I began to weep. This was the beginning.

Because I do not shed tears easily or often, I knew that while sitting at Brigit's Well I had been profoundly touched by spirit, and that it was time for me to do the work I had been resisting. But, for whatever reason, it took another year before I really got down to it.

One evening, after having a conversation with a friend about the various aspects and intricacies of ancestor reverence, I decided I was ready to turn and face that lurking shadow head on. "Okay," I said, "I'm going to try to work with this part of my ancestry—now what?" In this moment, she appeared in all her glory and brilliance—the goddess Brigit—and she said, "Start here. Start with me."

I knew some very basic things about the goddess Brigit spiritually, and I made a place for her on my main altar to connect with her on a regular basis. I also felt that it was important to have a more historical and mythological understanding of her, so I started to do my research. I began working daily with Brigit, and she immediately sent me seeking the history, the culture, and the traditions of the people who are known today as the Celts.

"Do not bother yourself with directly trying to connect with these men in your line that cause your heart anger and sadness," she told me. "Ancestry is deeper than that, and you do not need their stories to find what it is you are looking for. Go further back in time to the Ancient Ones, then learn what you can of the people's lore, their stories, their spirituality, their art, and their music. This is how you can begin to honor this part of your heritage."

And so I began. I spoke with those who had interest and knowledge in the history, story, song, and beliefs of the Celts. I found a priestess in the Celtic spiritual tradition and became her student. I read what I could find, I prayed, and I listened; and everywhere I went, I encountered the goddess Brigit again and again. In the Celtic mythology, she is one of the shining Tuatha dé Danann as poetess, sage, and daughter of the Dagda, the good god. In stories of the pre-Celtic primal goddess, she is the veiled hag, the *cailleach*. Again, in stories of the Roman invasion of Britain, the Brigantes, a Celtic tribe of northern England, fought under her as the martial goddess, Brigga.

One evening when I was in trance, Brigit appeared to me in serpent form. I took great interest in this, as many of the spirits I serve also have this aspect. I had never read or heard anyone refer to Brigit as a serpent goddess but, as I continued my studies, I eventually found that in Scottish lore she was associated with prophecy and known as the serpent queen. Brigit was so beloved by the Irish that the Catholic Church knew they were going to have a whole lot of trouble if they tried to get rid of this goddess. So we find her today still, in the symbology and mythology of Saint Bridget.

As my journey with this goddess continued through spiritual practice and research, I found her presence and lore in the most surprising of all places—Haiti, where the Celtic goddess and Christian saint was adopted, transformed into a *loa* (spirit) and placed in the Vodun pantheon.

"Maman Brigitte Li Soti Nan Anglete" or "Maman Brigitte she

comes from England" is the beginning of a song that was sung in ceremony to honor this powerful Vodou spirit. Maman Brigitte is a *ghede loa*, a *loa* that holds the powers of death, sexuality, and fertility. She is described as a bawdy old woman who guards the cemetery. She is a loa who heals the sick and protects women and children. Like other *ghede loas*, Maman Brigitte has a fiery tongue and is not shy about spouting obscenities. She drinks hot peppered rum and is legendary in her execution of the sexually suggestive *banda* dance. Along with her husband, Baron Semedi, Maman Brigitte is a guardian of the dead and leads them to the afterlife.

There is some dispute about the origins of this *loa*. The song I mention says she comes from England. Some say she is the Vodou manifestation of the Celtic Brigit, and that "She comes from England" simply means she is from the British Isles.

Following the English Civil War, thousands of Irish and Scottish men and women were deported, indentured, enslaved, and sent to the Caribbean islands by Cromwell's regime. And even before Cromwell's forced deportation, there were people from the British Isles immigrating to the Caribbean islands as indentured servants.

As Kerry Noonan has documented, Irish sailors arrived in the Caribbean as members of European navies; they fought on both sides of the Napoleonic wars, including the sea battles fought in the Caribbean by France and England. Many believe that in Haiti, the Irish shared their lore with the Africans and Brigit the saint was syncretized, becoming the new world *loa* known today as Maman Brigitte.

Others argue that this is unlikely. I have heard Pagans of European descent say, "The characteristics and behaviors of the *loa* are nothing like our lady Brigit's." In my experience, many white Pagans are afraid of and prejudiced against the religions of Africa and the Diaspora, and like to make it very clear that what they are doing spiritually is nothing like what "those people over there" are doing. I have heard white Pagans explain to someone that they are a Pagan or a witch, and then say, "But don't worry, I mean it's not Voodoo or anything." This could explain the resistance to any connection between the goddess Brigit and the *loa*.

There are Vodouists of African descent who understandably take issue with the idea of a spirit from Europe being one of the ancestral *loa* responsible for reclaiming the souls of their dead. And then there are folks from both sides who have no problem with the idea of the *loa* being syncretized with the saint or goddess, but agree that there is not enough evidence to say for sure, and that this belief is a new age romantic notion, at best.

Kenaz Filan, Vodou priest and author of the *Haitian Vodou Handbook*, says there was very little, if any, presence of Irish or English indentured servants in Saint-Domingue. He argues that, if there was a connection between the goddess and the *loa*, we would find Maman Brigitte being served in countries that had a higher percentage of indentured servants, such as Jamaica or Barbados.

Noonan, however, argues that:

> Priests from Brittany, the Celtic province of France, were present in Haiti both before its independence in 1804–05, and also since 1860, when Catholic priests again came to the country, for the Church had withdrawn its presence in Haiti in protest against the revolution. Catholics in both Ireland and Brittany are devoted to the Irish St. Brigit of Kildare, and many churches are dedicated to her in both areas. The influence of Irish settlers and sailors and Breton priests in spreading knowledge of St. Brigit in Haiti cannot be overstated.

People in both the Pagan and Vodou communities are concerned about spiritual appropriation, and believe that the attempt to make a connection between the goddess and the *loa* is just another way to sell Vodou to white Neopagans, or a way for white people, who in the past have been afraid of the religion, to find a way to comfortably fit in.

There are Vodou practitioners who will tell you that Maman Brigitte is usually syncretized with Mary Magdalene, who is seen kneeling and holding a skull, or with Saint Theresa, but not Saint Bridget. They will tell you that Maman Brigitte is not another manifestation of the Celtic Brigit, but of the Yoruba Orisha Oya who, like Maman Brigitte, is a guardian of the dead, rules the cemetery, and is also syncretized with

Saint Teresa. It is even more interesting to note that, in Santeria, Oya is also syncretized with our Lady of Candelaria and, like Brigit, her holy day is February 2.

I understand all sides of the argument. I personally don't believe Maman Brigitte's origins are in the British Isles or in West Africa. I believe her origins are in Haiti. She is a Haitian deity with roots clearly in Africa and with fairly convincing evidence that connects her to the British Isles. To me, she appears to be a combined manifestation of Oya, Brigit, and some other energy/spirit; she is a mystery that is unique to Haiti.

For me, the uncertainty around her origins is a reminder that the gods/goddesses and spirits are mysterious forces, and much more than what our limited human perceptions can imagine or comprehend. While on the surface, Brigit and Maman Brigitte may appear vastly different, both are associated with fertility and great powers of healing. I am also reminded that, in Scottish lore, Brigit is said to be two-faced: one side is the bright maiden's face of spring and life, while the other side is the dark hag's face of winter and death. This dark face of Brigit, the old woman who holds the mysteries of death and transformation, is who I can see in Maman Brigitte.

Regardless of her true origins, it was an especially magical experience to find that the goddess who showed up to help me deal with the ancestry I have as a result of slavery in America is possibly the same goddess who was converted to saint, transformed to *loa*, and today dances in a pantheon of spirits in a religion brought to Haiti by African slaves.

My work with Brigit has led me to believe, without a doubt, that she is a goddess intimately connected to the lives, experiences, and concerns of her children. When I call her in, she shows up; her energy is strongly felt and her presence unwavering. For me, the experience can sometimes feel overwhelming. Her immense power cannot be denied or dismissed. The visceral experience of her love is a force that continues to move and intrigue me. She is the sun of suns, the fiery arrow Breo-Saighit, illuminating all that is within and all that is without. She shines the light on the truth so that we may see the truth, know the truth, be the truth. Brigit keeps me in touch with the many truths, the paradox of truth.

I started my work with her focusing on truths that are hard, ugly, and painful. Over time, she guided me in discovering and integrating other truths—truths that hold great beauty and power.

I am a singer-storyteller inspired by the poetic spirits of *griots* as well as *bards**. I am a priestess-seer informed by spirits of Amengansie/Mamissiis (hereditary priestesses initiated to the African water spirit Mami Wata) and Hoodoo ladies, as well as Druids, *ovates**, and fairy doctors. I move through the world with courage, strength, pride, and perseverance, supported by spirits of the Amazons of Libya and Dahomey, as well as the Celtic women warriors of the British Isles. These spirits, along with many others connected to various lands and various ancestral traditions, all guide my steps and walk beside me. Carrying this truth in my heart, and speaking it at times, is how I've learned to honor all parts of my blood song.

With all that shared, I still cannot honestly say that I have come to an exact resolution or complete comfort when it comes to working directly with my ancestors of the Celtic lands. For me, in many ways, it is all still a process, and I do not know exactly where it will lead me. What I do know is that I can and will forever honor and celebrate this part of who I am by continuing my relationship with and devotion to the great goddess Brigit.

---

* Editor's Note: A *griot* is a West African storyteller, musician, or poet; a *bard* played a similar role in medieval Celtic culture. In ancient Druidic culture, an *ovate* was a prophet or seer.

REFERENCES:

Filan, Kenaz. 2006. *The Haitian Vodou Handbook: Protocol for Riding with the Lwa.* Rochester, VT: Destiny Books.

Foubister, Laura. 2003. *Goddess in the Grass: Serpentine Mythology and the Great Goddess.* Toronto: EcceNova editions.

Matthews, Caitlin.1997. *The Elements of the Celtic Tradition.* Dorset: Element Books.

Monaghan, Patricia. 1997. *The New Book of Goddesses and Heroines.* Minneapolis, MN: Llewellyn Publications.

Stewart, R. J. 2006. *Celtic Gods, Celtic Goddesses.* NY: Sterling Publishing.

Tan, Mambo Chita. 2012. *Haitian Vodou: An Introduction to Haiti's Indigenous Spiritual Tradition.* Minneapolis, MN: Llewellyn Publications.

Take Back the Hammer

Slippery Elm

with your white dress burning
with its hem of tangled gold
by the ring of naked oak at midnight
at the ecotone of ice and flower
you smile like an arsonist
before the match is lit

and what glimmering shadow flickers now
upon the mirror of my iris
and the contours of my nose and cheeks
as I behold a glorious hillside
blazing three hundred meters high
an open doorway   gobbling the air
from which re-emerge   laughing
as the heat   splits knots of wood
those tied wrongly to the tree
consumed in proud flame
who dance now unharmed
chanting canticles of liberation
and vibratory freshness!

no more the *malleus maleficarum!*
never more the torturous tongues of inquisitors!
no more the doors ripped from their threshings!

the hammer of the witches
        is the hammer of your forge!

O rippling clamorous mallet of mastery!
O concentric rings of indomitable change!
   blow the horn, beat the bodhrán!
   none can halt the stampede of spring!
none may quell the quickening green!
    Brigit, Brigit, mother of fire!
  I swear   by your wild red curls!
     by your so hot milk!
    by this hammer that is ours!

The Hem of Her Cloak: How Modern Brigit Worship Spread into the Southern Highlands of Appalachia

H. Byron Ballard

ere in the western mountains of North Carolina, on the buckle of the Bible Belt, we are building a goddess temple. With our wide and joyful feet, we will dance it into being in that intoxicating mixture of straw and sand and Southern red clay that is called "cob." It will sport a living roof and a stone foundation laid by the local Masonic order. There will be gardens, a bread oven in the yard, and composting toilets, because we are practical folk.

We understand that what we are doing is quite impossible, like the flight of a bumblebee. And yet, as our industrious fat friends do, we are finding ways to fly. How is this possible in Flannery O'Connor's "Christ-haunted landscape" of the rural South? Perhaps we cling to the hem of Brigit's cloak, for she is so present in this place, brought by her Scots-Irish lovers and their mothers and grandmothers.

Let me weave you a story, if I may.

In the ancient mountains of western North Carolina, in the southern highlands of Appalachia, many of us come from hardy—and poor—Scots-Irish stock, and we can succumb to the old cultural maladies of too much drink and too much temper. We can be stubborn and isolationist, but we can also be generous and welcoming.

We are a paradox, to be sure.

Many of us cling to the old harsh tenets of a Christianity that is proudly exclusive and no-nonsense—a religion that mourns births and rejoices at funerals. These spiritual practices range from simple foot washing and speaking angelic languages to dancing with venomous snakes. Within that framework is often found the cultural practices of an earlier and wilder people. The physical and spiritual healing techniques of our Celtic forebears blended with Cherokee herbalism to create a unique commingled spirituality, honored still in the remote fastnesses of rural counties. This wise-woman tradition is old folk magic practiced within the framework of this old-time mountain religion.

We approach life with this patchwork coat around us—our Celtic and Native cultural practices—which include the strangled grief of traditional mountain music, and this strong claim of spiritual rightness. Those of us who practice the earlier forms of Celtic spirituality examine the effects and meaning of the Gaelic diasporas. It is fitting that we turn away from the tribal people in our own land, though their folkways and deep roots are appealing, and dig into the cultural history that we've nearly forgotten.

We look eastward, to the lands from which our immigrant ancestors came. We break out the fiddles, we frequent Highland games, and we stand in ragged circles under a sickle of a moon. We absorb the collections of Carmichael and we study the lore and try to make sense of what was there before there was Catholic and Protestant, before there were Druids, when we lived in tribes of our own and were part of clans bound by kinship, by blood. Our nomad spirits look for different sorts of deities, our eyes glance away from the man on the cross and his stern, desert father.

We lean on our kinfolk, including our ancestors, and we look for different expressions of the divine. In my neck of the woods, we have turned, in several instances, to Brigit.

Who is she and who was she and how has she found such an outpouring of honor in this land far from the green fields of Ireland? We'll dive into that clear water and see what is to be seen beneath the surface of this sacred well of memory and lost desire.

The legends and tales spun round Ireland's Number Two Saint are numerous, charming, sometimes bizarre. How could it be otherwise? The older legends were adopted whole-cloth when she transitioned into a Christian holy woman and daughter of a Druid from her older guise as goddess of water, creativity, smith-craft, beer, dairy products, midwifery, fire, oats, brooms, honey, poetry, and healing.

As a saint, Bridget is remembered for her healing and spiritual leadership. One of the first convents in Ireland is attributed to her: a monastic center with women on one side and men on the other, led by the saint herself. She acquired the land for the monastic center, however, as only a goddess would; but we'll look at that story a little farther into our weaving.

Even though her hagiographies place her in the 5th century CE, there is also a story of young Bridget going into the barn to milk the cow and being whisked back in time, where she acted as midwife to the Blessed Virgin, bringing into the world her sacred son. One assumes she wiped her hands after swaddling the baby and returned to her own barn to finish the milking.

Immigrants came into my corner of the Appalachians from the north of Ireland in the 1700s. My own forebear on that side arrived in 1832, before An Gorta Mór, the Great Hunger that poured the wealth of Ireland into the wide reaches of the world. These dour Protestants would have flinched to think they were opening a doorway into the southern mountains, a doorway through which would step—in the 21st century, no less—a Catholic saint who is also a Pagan goddess.

Brigit belongs as much to us as to our sisters in Kildare town. She is the perfect goddess for mountain folk. She is resilient. She has a stout working knowledge of many disparate things. She is a *yarb* (herb) woman and a cove-doctor, knowing all the herbal remedies for all the mountain ills. She is fire and water and the broken, fresh earth of a hillside spring.

More years ago than I can remember, I read an article in a national Pagan magazine about a Pagan woman who traveled to Ireland and met with a Catholic sister who was a devotee of Saint Bridget. This chanced-upon story set me on a strange ramble. I set my sights on Ireland soon after, where I picked up a dented car in the port town of Dun Laoire and headed south to the home of Brigit, the sleepy town of Kildare town. In the original Irish, the town of Cill Dara (literally, the church of the oak) sits on a swath of land called the Curragh. It is a five thousand acre plain that serves as home to the Irish National Stud, where the thunder of heavy hooves is a regular occurrence in fields on which enormous Irish thoroughbreds graze.

We stayed in the same housing development as Sister Mary Minihan and her sister, Sister Rita, and we walked down to their little house on the off chance of meeting them. It was the beginning of a decades-long friendship between a Wiccan priestess and an Irish nun.

The experience of Kildare and Brigit, and the inspiration of the relighting of an eternal flame, was compelling and loaded with symbolism and import. I returned to the mountains, thoughtful about the spiritual nature of that ancestral place and how it jibed with my own land there in the southern highlands of Appalachia. Smelling vaguely of sheep poop and turf fires, I returned bearing a tiny bottle of water from Brigit's Well, and candles lit and *smoored* at her eternal flame.

That led me, in turn, to make my dedication to Brigit and to set the first and last part of that commitment in a land my ancestors left almost two centuries ago. And that veneration for a goddess-turned-saint brought me to a local spring and ruined springhouse made of stones, which those of us who love her have dedicated to her. We dress the spring with flowers and candles in her honor, remembering also the land spirits and the ancestors in the woods around it.

She is, all in all, a thoroughly magical and exemplary being who may have ridden westward with older ancestors in the vast Proto-Indo-European migrations. And millennia later, she migrated into the far corners of rural Appalachia. What followed was a pivotal event, a portal that opened on the next pathway.

Due in part to my own experiences in Ireland and to a Brigidine coven located in Asheville, my community held a public ritual in honor of the season. We didn't say it was Pagan or Wiccan, but billed it simply as a celebration of Brigit of Ireland, the gold-red woman. We adopted many of the traditional Irish parts of Brigit devotion, and our congregation included Pagans and goddess-worshippers, Catholic and Protestant Christians, and sundry folk of Irish extraction. One of the traditional parts of this celebration consists of pouring milk over a statue of Brigit. We invited the congregation to do that—to honor the woman and the spring and to be mindful of what they wanted to harvest in the new cycle. It took a long time, because those fifty people were hungry for time spent in that energy. They murmured prayers, they cried, they touched the statue and left some of their own pain and anxiety with this ancient symbol of healing and purification. There was fire and water and song and smoke. We prayed our prayers in patchy Gaeilge and tied *clooties*—those odd prayer flags—to a branch, and planted the branch near the old spring, where the request would be anchored in the place of healing and kept before the eyes of the spirit of the waters.

But the first Brigit sign in the hill country was the formation of Jill Yarnall's Brigit coven. Yarnall, a good Methodist girl from coal country, was a woman with similar deep and tangled mountain roots as my own, with a shared love for Irish Brigits. The group was formed "to honor a goddess that many in the group could relate to from personal heritage . . . in most covens, the idea of 'goddess' is fuzzy," she said. "Each woman comes to the circle with her own image of the goddess." Yarnall wanted a single focus for the corporate ceremonies of the group and to tap into what she called "the gestalt of the awakening of Brigit in order to give that some power."

The founding of The Mother Grove Goddess Temple in 2009 brought all these strings of love and history into a green and hallowed place. The temple brings together a broad cross-section of stakeholders that includes clergy and lay leaders, artists and designers, gardeners and herbalists.

Our vision is a sanctuary where people of all faith traditions may safely celebrate the divine feminine, a natural outgrowth of a thriving earth-religions community that must make do with ceremonies, rituals, and rites of passage held in public parks and rented halls. We are planning an environmentally sensitive building that incorporates the latest green technology, while fulfilling the requirements of the building codes for houses of worship. It will be sited on land that includes xeriscaping*, solar energy, and water-catchment systems, as well as outdoor gathering and worship space.

We are richly blessed with a growing pool of talented and passionate creators, willing to share their own talents with their community through this project. Annelinda Metzner created a concert in August, 2009 titled *In the Mother Grove* which began with a procession of drummers and

---

* Editor's Note: "Xeriscaping" is gardening or landscaping in ways that reduce the need for supplemental water from irrigation.

temple dancers and a powerful invocation of Astarte. The assembled audience participated in an ecstatic ritual that brought them to tears, reminding them of the thing they did not remember—that the goddess (however one names that divine energy) has been worshiped by women for more generations than we know. And she will be worshipped long after we are dust.

Mother Grove is not dedicated solely to Brigit, but in many ways she has laid the foundation for its building. The healing of community, the fire of poetry, the craft of dancing water, straw, and sand into a wall as strong as stone—she brings these skills to the people. She grounds us in our vision, giving us the gift of far-seeing. And yet she is ever practical, as a good countrywoman should be.

I returned to Kildare in 2003 and stood in the ruins of the old fire temple and made my personal dedication. I stood with two of my sister-priestesses and my young daughter, and said some simple words. And I felt the presence of scores of women around me, stretching out to the horizon—women who had stood here or in other temples and said the words of promise and praise and love, who made a commitment to something larger and deeper than themselves.

It has remained with me over the course of these long years—a promise of service that has grown into a community of people who are raising a goddess temple in the oldest mountains in the world, on the buckle of the Bible belt. We are like those fat bumblebees in the summer. We do the impossible (as we are often told). Our wings aren't strong enough, our bodies not built for flight. And yet . . . and yet . . . we fly.

For Brigit belongs to her Celtic people in America, too. Jill Yarnall told a lovely story that is tied to the older legend of the founding of the monastic center at Cill Dara. When Bridget went to the local chieftain to ask for a piece of land, he laughingly told her he'd give her all the land her cloak could cover. And so Bridget, wonder-worker, twirled her cloak from her shoulders—like a matador—and it covered acre after acre of the vast Curragh. There was land enough to build her double monastery and more for gardens. The chieftain was flummoxed but accepted that he had given his word. That is where the traditional story ends, but Yarnall added this grace note:

> As Bridget put her warm cloak back on, she tossed the edge over her shoulder. And that edge floated on the wind all the way to America, where it landed in the Appalachian Mountains.

Thus, she gave her green cloak a deep blue hem.

Even then, she claimed us and we are hers—warts, bad tempers, and all. We see her as a great blessing, whether we see her as goddess or saint or another Irishwoman who has the knack with herbs and knows her own mind. The wild and rugged tapestry that is the legacy of Brigit in these old mountains continues to beguile and to comfort us.

As you ramble these mountains and explore her ways, may it be so for you, as well.

REFERENCES:

Blethin, H. Tyler, and Curtis W. Wood. 1998. *From Ulster to Carolina*. Raleigh, N.C.: North Carolina Office of Archives and History.

Carmichael, Alexander. 1992. *Carmina Gadelica*. Great Barrington, MA: Lindisfarne Books.

Condren, Mary. 1989. *The Serpent and the Goddess*. San Francisco: HarperSan Franciso.

Lenihan, Eddie, and Carolyn Eve Green. 2003. *Meeting the Other Crowd*. New York: Tarcher.

Logan, Patrick. 1980. *The Holy Wells of Ireland*. London: Colin Smythe.

McCaffrey, Carmel, and Leo Eaton. 2002. *In Search of Ancient Ireland*. Chicago: Ivan R. Dee.

McMann, Jean. 1993. *Loughcrew: The Cairns*. Oldcastle, County Meath, Ireland: After Hours Books.

Monaghan, Patricia. 2003. *The Red-Haired Girl from the Bog: The Landscape of Celtic Myth and Spirit*. Novato, CA: New World Library.

Fa La La

Allison Stone

I want to celebrate Christmas,
my daughter announces. *I want*
blow-up things on the lawn.
She's wonderstruck by our neighbor's
inflatable Mickey Mouse elves.
Behind them, sunglass-wearing Santa, Frosty,
and Rudolph sway, arms around each other's shoulders.
Rudolph must have a leak; his snout's starting to pucker.
Daddy's family's Christian, so why can't we?
Across the street, plastic
snowflakes swirl in a giant sphere.
I try to set aside my filters—
tacky, money-driven, landfill-clogging kitsch—
to borrow my daughter's eyes and see, what?
Spectacle and pageant? Extravagant, in-your-face
celebration? No use. More than the forty years
between us, it's her nature I can't enter—
miles from my anxiety and distraction,
my husband's prickly Brooklyn edge.
No matter how many prayers I chant
or herbs I burn to Brigit,
how many full moon nights I step
onto the porch to wash my skin in silver,
she's the better Pagan—thirty-seven pounds
of joy receptors, songwriter of "Super Day"

and "I Love Everything."
Another neighbor's timer turns on,
makes bulbed reindeer graze. She grabs
my hand, tugs hard. Though it's cold
and dinner will be late,
I let her pull me toward the light.

Sacred Tattooing: A Dedication to Brigit

Phoenix Lefae

It was cold outside, with the dusk of early night just starting to settle over my town. I sat in a comfortable wooden chair surrounded by soft candlelight. I was nervous and excited for the event that was about to take place. I was about to take on a huge responsibility. I was ready to make a bold statement to the world, by stepping into a place in my spiritual life that I had never gone before.

A beautiful, calm priestess floated around me, getting all the preparations ready for the event. We did not normally work together spiritually, but I had known her for many years and trusted no one else to this ritual. My arm was resting on a table in front of me with my wrist facing up. Between the flickering of candles, in the sacred space my priestess friend had created, with the music playing in the background, I was in altered space ready for my dedication ritual to begin.

Finally, the priestess came to sit across from me, my arm serving as a barrier between the two of us. "You ready?" she said with a smile playing across her lips. I had never been so ready in all my life, but my nerves were keyed up and the words could not find their way to my mouth, so I nodded eagerly instead. Her own heavily tattooed arm lifted up the stencil of the Brigit's cross that she had created. I smiled as she gently placed the small shape of it on my wrist. When the stencil was transferred exactly where she wanted it, she looked up at me, smiling once again. "Here we go," she said. There was a feeling of anxiousness as I waited for the needle to pierce into my flesh.

I was giving myself to her, to Brigit. I was having her symbol forever embedded in my flesh. I was taking a step in my own evolution that many of my ancestors would have taken. There is some evidence that the ancient Celtic people, and those older than the Celts, including the Picts, used tattooing as a way to show their status. Many believe that the Druids had serpents tattooed on their arms as a visual expression of their spiritual achievements. Tattoos were given as a rite of passage, and different symbols demarcated which passages had been undertaken and completed. Warriors were tattooed in order to allow for recognition even if they were taken down on the battlefield. Tattoos were important and personal markers of identification.

My ancestors would not be familiar with the electric buzz that emanates from the tattoo machine. They would not recognize the little plastic cups of ink. They would not have had a stencil transferred onto their skin. But they would understand the dedication, the energy, the devotion, and, I hope, the ritual in which I was taking on this relationship with the Bright Flame herself.

The priestess turned on the tattoo machine and that familiar vibration filled the air, causing the tiny needles to quickly move up and down. She put the tip of her sacred tattoo machine into the black ink and brought it over to my arm. I took a deep breath and focused on the picture of the great goddess Brigit that we placed on the altar next to us.

It had taken several years to get me to this place of dedication. I had been a practicing eclectic Pagan for nearly fifteen years by this point. Prior to this night I had played with Bast, run through the forests with Artemis, traveled the realms with Morgan LeFae, and whispered in the night with Hecate. I love them all and cherish each connection, but never before had I felt ready to take the next step. Never before had I known that this was the right commitment for me to make. Never before had a goddess so clearly chosen *me*.

When the needle touched into my skin, the pain was not what I expected. This was not my first tattoo, but all my others are in places where I could not watch them being created. The pain and discomfort of this tattoo was lessened by the fact that I could watch the mark being placed on my wrist, by the fact that a dedicated priestess was going through the process with me, and most importantly by Brigit being called in to witness. I was being born in dedication to her.

I find Brigit to be one of the most well-rounded deities I have worked with thus far. She is a healer and midwife, a poet and artist, as well as a creator and warrior. She is often called Fiery Arrow, but she guards the sacred holy wells as well as the sacred holy flame. She is a goddess of the land, the sea, and the sky. She was so loved by the pre-Christian peoples that the Church made her into a saint and kept her holy day as a Christian celebration. There are goddesses all over the world that would not be ignored as Christianity started to take hold, and she is the one that comes from the land of my ancestors. She is the one whose song sings in my blood.

My first encounter with her was several years before my dedication ritual, during a trance where she called me "flame headed" and set me on fire. I didn't know what any of it meant at the time. The actions of a deity can be rather confusing, especially in trance. Her messages are not always clear, but now she calls to me like a moth to her forge flame. She is gentle and strong, humble and wise, patient and soothing. Looking back, the signs that I would end up working with her are innumerable, but hindsight is twenty-twenty.

Over the years, I have met many others dedicated to her. Each individual's experiences are different and unique. There are those that always find her to be a challenging goddess who pounds, beats, and molds them on her forge. There are those who always see her as a speaker of beauty, helping them to express their own beauty through words, music, and writing. There are those who connect to her healing powers and understand the depths of the well and the birthing of life.

All of these things are her magic. Whether she works from the forge, from the well, or in the oratory, her work in the world, and with her priestesses, is done with love and compassion.

My personal dedication ritual took only a half an hour. Small black line connecting to small black line formed a beautiful piece of her forever on my skin. It took longer to set the sacred space than do the sacred working, but afterwards I felt elated. My energy level was vibrating at a high rate and I felt a fire in my head like I often do after an encounter with Brigit. I was standing at a new beginning, a beginning of my life as a priestess of Brigit.

I understood this was only the beginning, but I had no idea where this work would lead me.

As our relationship has grown, I have started to know her as the warrior. A lesser known image of Brigit as warrior is often connected to her under the name Brigantia. In this guise, she is the energy of the sun, the heat of the fire, and the aggression of the boar. Unlike other warrior goddesses who enjoy the fight and blood spill of battle, who relish their opportunity to pick over the slain, Brigit is a warrior who understands the true cost of war and laments for those who have given their lives. It is because of the warrior goddess offering her lamentation to the wounded and the fallen that Saint Bridget was named Mary of the Gael, believed by some to be the foster mother of Jesus. And it is through her worship as a saint that the shape of Brigit's cross comes to us.

The origins of Brigit's cross are most likely the pagan sunwheel but, again, this information has been lost. It was believed to help protect a house from fire in ancient times, and the Christians believe that this symbol was used to convert Saint Bridget's pagan father at the time of his death. To me, it is a symbol of her divine protection, her divine inspiration, and her divine touch. Although the initial meaning may have been lost, this symbol represents the energy of Brigit in all her magical forms to many modern Pagans and Christians.

I proudly wear this energy on my body and, in many ways, this connection helps me to make a bridge for those on the Pagan side of the landscape and those on the Christian side. Although I have no Christian background, through my connection to Brigit I am able to explain my worship as a Pagan to those who are not of my faith. From my connection to her, I am able to find commonality with those whose beliefs are different from my own. That commonality brings a deeper understanding and, more often than not, acceptance.

I believe that the modern guise of Brigit is that of peacemaker and mediator. I have watched her symbol be a way to bring disparate cultures together with understanding and clarity. The mark on my arm serves as a personal touchstone. When I find myself in conflict, when I am searching for the right words, when I need to connect to compassion, or send out a prayer for healing, I can touch the cross on my arm and connect to her.

A loving priestess put this symbol on my body. And through this simple magical act I have been able to more easily find my connection to Brigit. The goddess herself continues to show me a path to myself—a path to who I truly am.

REFERENCES:

Bladey, Conrad. 2000. *Brigid of the Gael: A Complete Collection of Primary Resources.* Hutman Productions: Linthicum, MD.

Maria, Tania. 2011. *Spiritual Skin: Sacred Tattoos: More Than Skin Deep.* CreateSpace Independent Publishing Platform: www.createspace.com.

Skye, Michelle. 2010. *Goddess Alive!: Inviting Celtic & Norse Goddesses into Your Life.* Llewellyn Publications: St. Paul, MN.

Brigit's Light: A Break from Rain

Kersten Christianson

To remind us of her presence,
the sun opens her blinds
occasionally.
She dusts the glass-beaded crystals
waiting in windows
and washes my space in gold. .
She travels across hushed waters
slipping silently into the sea.

INSPIRATION AND INVOCATION: CREATING A RITUAL WITH BRIGIT

Betz King

There is no *need* to invent a Brigit ritual—many fine ones already exist. But rituals that are created, rather than inherited, offer a personalized, embodied experience of the goddess in a way that following someone else's "ritual recipe" cannot. Since one of the faces Brigit wears is that of the patron of the arts, surely she would bless the creation of a ritual seeking her council.

From the Latin *rītuālis*, for "rite" or "ceremony," rituals have been present since the beginning of time and across all cultures as an integral part of religious, spiritual, political, social, and family life. Rituals help us to embody symbolic expressions of our inner life and search for meaning. What need is greater than the need to make meaning of life? This search for meaning has been expressed over and over in the mythologies of humankind, prompting Radha Parker to call myth and ritual "the vehicles through which the value-impregnated beliefs and ideals that we live by, and live for, are preserved and transmitted."

Rituals, like homing beacons, help us to find our way home. They provide many psychological benefits as well. A comprehensive review of fifty years of research on the psychological use and importance of ritual by Barbara Fiese and her colleagues at Syracuse University finds rituals to be " . . . powerful organizers of family life, supporting its stability, and increasing both personal identity and marital satisfaction." Ritual can play a noble role, protecting and nurturing a group of people, helping each member to self-actualize and to learn to love deeply. Sadly, many powerful rituals have been claimed as the property of various religions, and those that are left over are often so watered down that their original,

magical intentions are too weak to be effective. Personalized rites, based
on the composition and need of the members, return rituals to their more
powerful origins.

Rituals follow a very simple recipe. They have an opening, a
verb/intention, and a closing. The opening generally serves to create
sacred or liminal space, and to raise some energy that will be directed
toward the verb/intention. The verb/intention is the most important part,
as it is the place where the action and magic of the ritual occurs. The
closing generally serves as a time for gratitude, dissolution of any energies still present, and a return to regular, non-sacred space.

Clarity regarding the intention of the ritual will help with the choice
of the ritual verb. Imber-Black and Roberts, who have studied rituals for
much of their career, suggest five common ritual verbs: relating, changing, healing, believing, and celebrating. These broad categories of rituals
may include rites of blessing, cursing, worshiping, invoking, banishing, pacifying, energizing, imbuing, consecrating, and transforming, to
name but a few. Psychodrama teachers, such as Adam Blatner, caution
that a good ritual must combine "hypnosis and drama . . . effectively
evoking images, memories and ideas that are most appropriate for the
experience." The stimulation of all five senses is encouraged whenever
possible, as each of our senses follows its own path back to the archetypal
experiences of our ancestors. This allows for the use of music, incense,
food, fabrics, and special altar items. Once the ritual intention is chosen,
it must be made manifest within the ritual. For example, the ritual
intention of banishing would be made symbolically by letting a helium
balloon float away. The ritual intention must have a concrete physical
expression in the ritual; it is the climax of the ritual and the focal point of
the energies that are raised in the opening portion of the ceremony.

A ritual accessing the goddess Brigit begins like any other ritual,
with the choosing of the ritual intention. Her feast day of Imbolc celebrates the awakening of spring and is a good time to seek blessings
for new pursuits, but this is not the only time Brigit can be invoked. As
a triple goddess of healing, smith-craft, and creativity, Brigit has many
powers to choose from; they can all be considered transformative
energies. She can be called on to help a woman become a mother,

calibrate a magical tool, or inspire a work of art. Baby showers are a very watered-down version of a Brigit blessing ritual, the ritual verb/intention being to bless the new life. New students of the magical arts often take their vows on Brigit's feast day, with the ritual intention of transforming their egoic personalities into soulful tools of healing for the world. This author dedicated a weekend campsite to Brigit while writing this article, creating and hanging an eye of the goddess above the writing table, and writing only while the campfire (of inspiration) was burning.

Let's work with the first example: a blessing ritual for a pregnant, first-time mother. The intention, to bless the woman's transformation, must be made tangible. Brigit's symbols can be used throughout the ritual to physically, psychologically, and spiritually express this transformational blessing. Symbols, the oldest form of communication known to humankind, allow something small and simple to represent something quite epic. Symbolism is key to the creation of a good ritual. Perhaps the simplest yet most powerful symbol associated with Brigit is the element of fire. Her name translates as "bright one" and, in ancient times, she was worshiped as a fire goddess at her sacred shine in Kildare. Brigit blesses the fires of the home hearth, the fires of the forge, and the fires of creative inspiration. Water is another of Brigit's symbols, as she has long been associated with sacred wells and the waters of inspiration and healing. The image of an eye, also attributed to Brigit, offers wonderful symbolism related to clear vision and being watched over or protected. It can be represented by Brigit's iconic straw crosses or by colorful, yarn-wrapped crosses known as "eyes of the goddess." Each of these symbols lend themselves beautifully to a blessing ritual.

Ritual symbols are often displayed on an altar of some sort, often in the center of a real or imaginary circle, which will be designated as sacred space during the opening of the ritual. Candles and a lovely chalice full of mountain or mineral water lend themselves well to an altar for Brigit.

The simplest ritual opening might involve a formal procession into the room, followed by a prayer invoking Brigit's presence, or a song with a similar intention. Other common ritual openings include the verbal invocation of the four directions, four elements, or four facets of the goddess (maiden, mother, queen, and crone) done by an officiating high priestess or by other ritual participants. Ritual cleansing of the space and or participants may be done with incense or sprinkled water at this time, as well.

Once sacred space has been established, Brigit can be invoked and invited in. Poetic invocations are often used because they are easy to remember and can be recited with increasing speed and volume (usually three times) as a method of raising the energy in the room. They need not rhyme. An invocation might draw on references to fire and water . . .

> Brigit, keeper of the flame
> transform the dark to light;
> Brigit, keeper of the well
> Wash our fears away.

. . . or to Brigit's areas of specialty . . .

> Brigit, healer, blacksmith, muse . . .

The most important ingredient in an invocation is its enthusiasm; it has to feel right.

Once sacred space has been created and Brigit has been invoked, the ritual intention of transforming the mother-to-be can take place. A simple and powerful way to make the mother's transformational intent into something concrete might involve the use of candles that will remain lit in some format until the after the mother's labor. Guests might be asked to write possible obstacles to a peaceful labor and birth on magician's flash paper, and then offer them for transformation into Brigit's flames. Or each guest might hold the chalice of healing water from the altar and put wishes and blessings into it. The mother-to-be might drink the water during the ceremony or save it until she is in labor. The gathering community could make colorful goddess eyes and Brigit's crosses to hang in the delivery room, so that the goddess can watch over her delivery. Beads that are strung on a necklace could represent blessings. All who attend the rite could be woven together with yarn around their wrists, each vowing to wear the yarn until after labor is complete, and each vowing to lend the mother and child strength, peace, and courage during the time of transformation. This is the climax of the ritual, where creativity enters; and, as the realm of creativity also belongs to Brigit, there is no shortage of expressions. The only requirement for this part of the ritual is that it makes sense to the mother-to-be and that she has something tangible to take with her from the ritual and into her labor.

The closing of the ritual is often very similar to the opening. It's time to say goodbye to Brigit for now. But not to worry, she is never far away. Prayers of thanksgiving might be made, and any energies invoked should be released with gratitude and reverence. It is also good to eat something to assist with the return to normal consciousness; feasting allows for further, less-formal celebration in Brigit's name.

Writing a ritual with an opening, a verb/intention, and a closing is not difficult. Ritual is the ballroom in which we dance with the gods and goddesses. When Brigid is called into the room via a ritual that has been personally inspired and designed, she comes ready to dance. Then the goddess is alive and magic is afoot.

REFERENCES:

Blatner, A. 2000. "A New Role for Psychodramatists: Master of Ceremonies." *International Journal of Action Methods*. Summer: 86–93.

Campbell, J. 1949. *The Hero with a Thousand Faces*. New Jersey: Princeton Press.

Fiese, Barbara H., et al. 2002. "A Review of 50 Years of Research on Naturally Occurring Family Routines and Rituals: Cause for Celebration?" *Journal of Family Psychology* 16 (4): 381–390.

Fisher, M. 1999. "Soul Pain and the Therapeutic Use of Ritual." *Psychodynamic Counseling* 5 (1): 53–72.

Houston, J. 1987. *The Search for the Beloved: Journeys in Mythology and Sacred Psychology*. New York: Putnam.

Frankl, V. 1984. *Man's Search for Meaning*. New York: Simon & Schuster.

Imber-Black, E., and J. Roberts. 1992. *Rituals for Our Times*. New York: HarperCollins.

Jung, C. G. 1964. *Man and His Symbols*. New York: Doubleday.

May, R. 1991. *The Cry for Myth*. New York: Norton.

Moore, T. 1992. *Care of the Soul*. New York: HarperCollins.

Parker, Radha. 1999. "The Art of Blessing: Teaching Parents to Create Rituals." *Professional School Counseling* 2 (3): 218–225.

Parker, R. et al. 1996. "A Typology of Ritual: Paradigms for Healing and Empowerment." *Counseling and Values* 40 (2): 82–97.

THE STORY OF BRIGIT: A CONVERSATION

Ita Roddy

Saint Bridget was a feminist, there's many'll vouch for that,
Converted pagans, it was said, with rushes from a mat.
Travelled in a chariot, visiting the poor,
Built a convent, a monastery, a cathedral with two doors.

What sort of feminist? I never heard the like!
Sure Feminism wasn't invented 'til long after the bike.
Bad cess to her converting, isn't religion now a curse,
With half the population—more—voting for divorce.
And as for driving chariots, she'd never hold the reins,
And whoever saw a woman, saint or no saint, fitting drains.

About her early days I haven't much to say
Except to note how generously she gave Dubhthach's sword away.
Dubhthach was her father—Chieftain, Druid, Lord,
And wasn't very pleased with the loss of that same sword.
So when Bridget came to marry, he duly picked the groom,
As was the ancient custom in that age of doom and gloom.
A poet of the highest rank, he brought to her one day,
But little Biddy shook her head, smiled and said "no way!"
I'd rather go a-travelling down south where all is fair,
And so she left Faughart and landed in Kildare.
Not the first to shy of marriage, I'll certainly grant you that,
But the first to hit the Curragh not looking for 'the Flat'!

Most likely 'twas the poet she didn't want to wed;
What woman wants a muse or two beside her in the bed?
But if it's true she hit the road and headed for Cill Dara—
No better place to find a man—a soldier tall or jockey small,
A "Lily White'"will spend the night with any woman, stout or light
If she's in funds, begorra!

So sad to meet a one-tracked mind,
Who thinks so little of womankind.
To have a man may be a pleasure
But not the only kind of treasure.
Our Bridget came to that great plain
In search of something less mundane:
A place to live and love and pray,
To meet the Eastern sun each day.
And look out on her church of oaks
A sanctuary for poorer folks.
Where bed was offered and a chat,
A refuge bright to hang your hat,
And beer three times a day to cheer
Each lonely beggar who appeared.
To talk so much of charity,
Is dangerously close to vanity.
I fail to understand a woman
Born to wealth who turns out common.
Rejects silver, gold, precious jewels,
But then there are all sorts of fools—
Rich in pocket, poor in mind,
Who do not care for kith or kind.
There usually is some kind of blemish
That turns them from the path of marriage,
Pock-marked, short-legged or bosom-empty.

I fear your Bridget suffered plenty.
What Bridget looked like doesn't matter,

I wish you'd stop your idle chatter.
Now to get back to number one
Our woman was no dim-witted son.
The King of Leinster found this out,
When he with magisterial clout
Offered to build her church of oak
On land the measure of her cloak.
Bridget accepted and went away,
Came back just six months to the day
With home-spun shawl of web-like thread
And spread it just as he had said—
Upon the Curragh far and wide.
And there it stretched a crimson tide—
Miles and miles of miraculous substance.
So now you see she had abundant
Brains, insight, creativity,
Perception, wisdom, femininity.

A "cute hoor" is what I'd say,
On the make both night and day.
Because her father was a chieftain,
Kings and bishops she kept meeting.
Opportuning them for land and money,
Since she was raised on milk and honey
Unlike most women of that age—
I spell it out upon this page:
Bold of limb—brazen of face
Your Bridget didn't know her place!

Wrong again in your presumption!
I wonder where you get the gumption
To continue with this moral slander,
When it's clear to all—you just can't stand her.
In that dark age when might was right
She took to heart a woman's plight—

'Twas said her mother did inspire her
Raised her up and then released her.
Brocessa, bondswoman—a slave it seems
Filled her head with freedom's dream.
And so she urged young woman all
To follow her and heed the call
Free in body, free in soul, liberty for woman
Now there's gall!
No more torture, no more terror
No more masters, no more error.
Let us sisters join together
Bonds of home and mind to sever
And learn to live as was intended
In pious retreat, all fear suspended.

Turned women's heads, is what you're saying,
Taught reading, writing—not much praying.
Took maidens from their world confined
From home and hearth and family kind.
Put them in community
To languish—in perpetuity.
No men allowed within the gates
In church divided from their mates.
A life unnatural you must agree
It's married, women are born to be.

I understand you feeling thus,
No need a *ghrá** for such a fuss.
A choice in life was what she offered
Either, or, our Bridget proffered.
Wife, mother, nun, preacher,

---

* Author's Note: "Lily Whites" are the GAA (Gaelic Athletic League, or Irish football) team for Kildare; the "Pale" is the area around Dublin formerly entirely controlled by the English; *ghrá* means "love."

Sower, reaper, healer, teacher.
To choose is such a pleasant thing
While force has a discordant ring.
Signs on the female population
Responded to her invitation.
Three thousand flocked to her wattle church
Left all behind them in the lurch.
Throughout the land her following grew
Until it numbered quite a few.
Thirteen thousand is what they say—
Not bad for a team, even today.
Dublin Blue or Lily White
I'm sure their managers would delight
If they could muster on the Pale
As many as "Mary of the Gael."

Bridey: From Personal to Global

Aline O'Brien (M. Macha NightMare)

blue moon shines in the sky over northern California, as witches gather in a large room lit only by the candlelight from altars in each quarter. In the center stands a table dressed in lace, greenery, and fresh white flowers. Upon the table sits a brass-trimmed stainless-steel bowl shining in the firelight—Brigit's Well. Inside the bowl is a cauldron; surrounding the bowl are three large white pillar candles; and nearby is an anvil and hammer.

Three priestesses of Brigit—one wearing red, one gold, and one white—embody her and speak in her voice. Tonight, I wear red. As I speak of her, then speak to her, then speak in her voice, I feel my heart open. I walk around the circle and look into the eyes of each person. I feel her smiling through me, feel her palpably when I touch the hands or heart of every celebrant.

I listen to Brigit's words spoken by my sister priestesses and myself. We speak of the year just passing. We all—celebrants and priestesses—review our lives of the year just passing. We return to the present with our plans for the coming year. The priestess in gold lights the cauldron and, as its flames arise, she invites each of us to approach Brigit's altar and make a public pledge of our goal for the coming year. What promise will we make to Brigit? What blessing will we seek? What service will we do? What creative project? What inspiration or powers or healing do we ask of her?

We may commune silently or we may speak our pledge aloud in community. Most of us speak aloud. As each pledge is spoken, Brigit of the forge strikes her anvil to seal it.

I approach the altar and feel the heat of the fire. I reach into the warm waters surrounding her flaming cauldron, draw them out and anoint my face, neck, arms, and chest. I ask Brigit to bless my writing with her inspiration. I ask Her to guide my fingers on the keyboard. I hear the ring of metal striking metal as I take a little yellow glittery birthday candle from a small basket on the altar and light it with the flame from one of the pillar candles, taking Brigit's light back into my life, into my work.

On the World Wide Web, I have found a shrine to Brigit called Ord Brighideach (www.ordbrighideach.org/), an online sister- and brotherhood of people who honor Brigit. This unique devotional order came about by way of a website created by two women in Oregon. The Order is comprised of nineteen cells, like the nineteen priestesses of Brigit at Kildare, with nineteen people in each cell. Each cell is named for a tree, and each day, beginning at sundown, one of the nineteen tends Her flame; on the twentieth day, as of old, Bridey herself tends it. Some of the cells also maintain a Web presence, by creating a website or setting up a listserv to share experiences, insights, recipes and stories, or all. There's also a listserv for the entire order, subscription being optional. All websites are linked to the main Order.

The process is that, when a dedicator joins the Order, she or he sends a small donation to the keepers of the flame in Oregon—that is, the people who created the website and set up the order. In return, she or he receives a blessing for flame-keepers (a prayer), and a candle lit from the Kildare flame with which to start her or his flame-keeping.

I had known of the order for a few years, visited the site, and reflected on whether I wanted to join. The site invites those who hear her call to join in shared devotionals:

If She speaks to you—as poet, healer, smith, storyteller, musician, craftsperson, midwife, mother, hearth keeper, land steward, tender of herds, seer, woman of fire, lawgiver, deity of

the home, lady of the sun, or simply as goddess or saint—you
are welcome to walk among us.

So I contemplated for a while, going back to the site from time to
time and listening for her call.

Now Brigit is a goddess I can relate to: she is brilliant, powerful,
compassionate, tender, and easy to approach. She displays strength, skill,
industry, and artistry in ways that don't threaten men and don't restrict
women. To the strong woman, she models righteous strength. To the
independent woman, Brigit needs no partner to make her whole. Many
people all over the world can hear her singing.

My reservation about joining was that I travel erratically and I
wondered how I could maintain my watch in airports, buses, cars, and
wherever I was lodging. I knew that I was expected to tend her flame
once every twenty days, for as long as possible, taking safety into consideration. The principle is that the longer we are able to tend, the more
energy we will be able to generate—an offering to this world and the
otherworld, as well as to Brigit,"She Who Gives Energy."

I set aside my reservations, confident that I could somehow maintain
my pledge and keep my watch.

When we dedicators apply to join the Order, we commit to keeping
Brigit's flame for one solar year. We are asked to swear an oath to Brigit
as a flame-keeper the first time we tend the flame. The oath includes
a statement of dedication to Brigit and to our commitment to tend her
flame faithfully, reflecting our own path to her service.

Often my life is such that I feel my knowledge of what Brigit has
to offer me comes from time spent dancing in the heat of her forge. She
powers the blows that shape me. She is the annealer of my soul. Yet I see
her in the greening earth after winter's dark. In the coastal hills where
I live, I see wild iris spring up in her footsteps. She pours the waters of
healing. She stirs the cauldron of compassion. She keens in grief for the
dead and whistles up the wind. She is balm to my soul.

These are the things I spoke of when I first pledged myself to the
Order.

When I first joined the Order, I chose an all-woman cell and thus became a sister of the Laurel, a member of Cill Labhras, tending the fourteenth shift. One member of our cell designed a Laurel Cell website to help establish our group identity. My cell sisters were witches, Pagans, Christians, liberal and conservative, conventional and unconventional. What we shared is our dedication of maintaining the sacred flame of Brigit bright throughout the world.

After keeping the fourteenth shift of Cill Labhras for several years, I lapsed. In the meantime, the Order underwent some internal changes, and so did I. The Order now has its own domain and a new website, with shift calendars, sample pledges, prayers, songs, and a discussion forum. I have rejoined the Order, on a blue moon when I was ready to refocus my life. I have rededicated myself to keeping Brigit's flame as an individual flame keeper unconnected to a cell.

In the fire-lit room in California, we have stood before Brigit's Holy Well and sacred flame and spoken pledges to her. We've felt on our skin the healing waters of Her Well and of the waters of the world. We've taken small candles, lit from the altar candle, which had been lit from the Kildare flame. We've heard the ringing of hammer on anvil.

Now we come together singing a chant. I take up a woven-grass Brigit doll, dressed all in white lace and flowers, and hold her aloft in my left hand. I reach back my right hand to grasp the left hand of the next priestess. One by one everyone joins hands and we chant and dance the spiral. We follow the Brigit dolly, winding inward to a tight spiral in the center; then we turn and face each person, one by one. Looking at the fire of Brigit in each pair of eyes, we spiral outward to the perimeter of the sacred space. Then turn and turn in again, seeing each face, tightening the dance into a corkscrew near the center; turn and out again. We dance the spiral in and out and in again, all the while chanting Starhawk's famous chant:

We will never, ever lose our way to the well of Her memory
And the power of Her living flame, it will rise, it will rise again,
Like the grasses, through the dark, through the soil to the sunlight,
We will rise again.

When the time is right, we raise our arms aloft and change the chanting to a wordless sound coming from deep in our hearts through wide open throats, louder and higher as our collective energy builds, until it crests and showers back down upon us. We slowly sink to the floor. We touch our hands and foreheads to the ground, imbuing our pledges with the energy we raise in the dance, as we seal the spell with these words from the *Carmina Gadelica*:

What we have received tonight has been held in our keeping.
What passes now flows out of our hands and into the Earth,
Trusting in time and right season,
Let us go on.

Every year in early February, I have renewed my connection to Brigit and made a pledge to her in the presence of the sisters and brothers in my local community.

Now, once every twenty days, I join with others who hold Bridget dear in keeping her sacred flame. Beginning at sundown, as in the Celtic counting of nights and days, we light a candle to her. All 300 of us flame-keepers do this from wherever we live in the world, in twelve countries: Australia, Brazil, Canada, Finland, Greece, Ireland, Netherlands, New Zealand, South Africa, Spain, the United Kingdom, and the United States of America. We honor our heritage as we take it into the age of the Internet.

In our annual ritual in honor of Brigit in California, and in our keeping of her sacred flame, we reconstruct the ways of our ancestors in our high-tech, multi-cultural, post-modern world. We carry Brigit's light of consciousness through the darkness and into the future.

REFERENCES:

Carmichael, Alexander. 1992. *Carmina Gadelica: Hymns and Invocations*. Great Barrington, MA: Lindisfarne Books.

BRIGIT

Annie Finch

Ring, ring, ring, ring! Hammers fall.
Your gold will all be beaten
over sudden flaming fire
moving from you, the pyre. Sweeten
your cauldron, until the sun
runs with one flame through the day
and the healing water will sing,
linger on tongues, burn away.

Fire Will Make It Whole

Sabina Magliocco

Field notes: February 17, 1995

The ritual starts late, like all Pagan events. About a hundred people are gathered in a large conference ballroom in a San Jose hotel; chairs are arranged all around the walls and people sit, some uneasily, some talking in groups, laughing, gossiping. Starhawk, a plump, middle-aged woman in a loose print dress, leggings, and incongruous red ankle socks, stands near the room's center where a pile of scarves has been placed. She tests the sound system, confers with others, finally begins to call the rag-tag assembly to order and explain the purpose of the ritual: to find what is most sacred to us, what we most deeply value.

She begins by asking us to imagine that we are trees rooted in the soil, our roots reaching deep into the earth's molten core, our branches drawing down the moon's shining light, cool silvery energy meeting hot, fiery energy in our beings. When we are all grounded and centered, the quarters are called and she calls the goddess as Brigit and the god as the greening god, the Green Man, Dylan Thomas's "force that through the green fuse drives the flower," calling him through redwood, oak, artichoke, zucchini, and garlic into our midst:

Greening god, redwood god;
Greening god, artichoke god . . .

She drums, while we sway and dance. Some take up scarves in the center and dance around us, waving them. One smiling young man comes towards me waving a scarf and we dance awhile, twirling and twisting to the drumming and chants. Finally, our voices reach a crescendo—and then fall silent.

Now Starhawk is taking us on a guided meditation to find the sacred. She asks us to form small, intimate groups where we can talk about it. A small group of us join hands to form a ring. I follow Starhawk's words and find myself walking along a path to a dark wood, and I think of the words from Dante's *Inferno* that my father used to recite to me:

Nel mezzo del cammin di nostra vita
Mi ritrovai per una selva oscura
Che la diritta via era smarrita

In the middle of our life's journey
I found myself in a dark wood
Having strayed from the straight and narrow.

I think of how, in the last year, I, too, have seemingly lost my way unexpectedly in the middle of my life's journey. I feel like I've jumped off the edge of a precipice; I'm hanging in mid-air, waiting to see whether I fall or am held aloft.

Now Starhawk is asking us to contact the holy of holies, what we consider sacred. Several images flash before me in response to her words—my connection with nature, my love for animals, some inner core of strength and integrity I seek—only to be discarded as the real center of my life unfolds: my work, my teaching, my writing, and my efforts to convey to my students not only other peoples' and cultures' basic humanity, but their own as well. As Starhawk speaks of the difficulties, the obstacles to achieving one's goal, I feel as though she has already thought my thoughts. She asks if Brigit has us on her anvil and is tempering us in her fire, making us sharper, beating us with her hammer as she clamps us in her tongs, and I think of my struggles during the past several years: my frustrated search for a tenure-track position, my troubled relationship with my Sardinian field site, and my failed marriage. Tears run down my face and drip onto my chest; in my thin dress, I shiver with grief and cold.

Now we are sitting on the floor and we're supposed to share our idea of the sacred with the group. I open my eyes and realize I am not the only one weeping. One by one, the members of my circle speak of their families, their children; as my turn approaches, I begin to feel selfish for considering my work sacred. But, somehow, I manage to blurt it out and, somehow, blessedly, the others don't get up and leave in disgust or chastise my arrogance, but gather round me and support me.

Now another guided meditation takes us to the forge where Brigit is tempering us on her anvil, shaping us. Another forest path, another clearing: this time I recognize the road that goes down to the valley below Monteruju, the town in Sardinia where I did fieldwork, and a clearing under a live oak tree where a woman is working at a forge. Her hair forms a fiery red halo around her; her white raiment is embroidered with living leaves and tendrils; her golden eyes burn into mine. I bring her a gift: it is my heart, broken in pieces, swollen and bloody like meat from a butcher shop. She takes that heart and puts it into her forge, heating it till it's white hot; then she beats it with her hammer. The blows resound through my whole body, and with each stroke I shudder in pain.

"This is your heart, and fire will make it whole," she says, as her eyes burn through me once again. She takes that red-hot heart and slips it into my chest, where its heat spreads through my reptile-cold body.

Then she takes up her tools again and makes a sharp pocketknife and a pen, which she cools in her sacred well and hands to me. And now she directs me to drink from that well, and I do. I find myself at the spring of Funari near my Sardinian field site; E. T., my friend and key informant, is walking up the path with me back to the real world.

In the conference room, we dance the spiral dance as we chant in harmony:

We will never, lose our way to the well of her memory
And the power of the living flame it will rise, it will rise again!

Our voices, spiraling in unison, grow ever more intense; the dance, as always, pulls us along, dragging the whole community in front of us so that we all see one another, as the old world circle dances do at festivals and celebrations. For the first time, I really feel the "cone of power," which Pagans are always talking about, rising from us all, from our combined voices and tears. It rises through the ceiling of the hall and onward, upward to the heavens. The energy is grounded, and at last the circle is uncast and opened.

That was my first experience of the goddess Brigit as I wrote it in my field journal (the record of field research kept by all folklorists and anthropologists) after attending a Reclaiming* ritual for the first time at PantheaCon in 1995. It changed my life in unexpected and profound ways.

On the most basic level, it taught me what Pagans mean when they speak of ritual as transforming consciousness. While I had been studying modern Paganism for a few years already, and had heard a number of people tell me that the purpose of rituals was to change consciousness, I had always interpreted that to mean that rituals raised consciousness about social and political issues—which, of course, they do. What had escaped me until this point was that they do so by inducing alternate states of consciousness in which participants can experience a different reality.

This understanding reshaped my research: I understood my Pagan interlocutors on a much deeper and more personal level because I, too, had undergone an extraordinary experience. I began to focus more on how rituals generate alternate states of consciousness, how ritualists learn the skills to create these art pieces, and how good rituals allow participants to interweave the ritual narrative with their own experiences and memories to generate an inner state filled with deeply personal meaning.

On a more intimate level, my experience of the goddess Brigit transformed me by granting me a feeling of great comfort during a fraught and anxious period in my life. Not having grown up with any religious training, I lacked a belief in a personal deity who took an interest in

---

* Editor's Note: For a definition of Reclaiming, visit www.reclaiming.org/about/directions/definition.html.

humans as individuals, who watched over us and guided our choices in life, and to whom we could turn for guidance and succor. I felt intrinsically that nature was sacred, and took solace in the rhythm of the seasons and the vastness of the universe, knowing that my problems were insignificant in the larger scheme of things and that they all would pass in cyclical fashion.

This self-made philosophy made me sympathetic towards Paganism, but it lacked any sense of the divine as a subjective presence. As a teenager, I had once sacrificed to Minerva, the Roman goddess of victory and wisdom, at a church in Assisi that had once been her temple; my sacrifice was a bunch of wild flowers, which I left under the portico of the church in order to do well on a national Latin exam. I received the second-highest score. But as I left adolescence behind, I also forsook the notion of gods and goddesses as childish, part of the Classical past in which I had immersed myself through study, but which had nothing to do with my everyday life.

The appearance of the goddess Brigit in my vision re-opened a door that I had thought long closed. I felt perhaps there was some force watching over me, that my life had purpose and meaning, and that the derailment in my life's plans I had experienced might have a role I could not yet perceive.

The core of the vision was the reforging of my heart and the goddess's words, "This is your heart, and fire will make it whole." They held special meaning. Not only did Brigit heal my heart, transforming a bloody, broken mess into something whole, healthy, and glowing; she also indicated that this healing would take place through the element of fire, which I knew was associated with passion, courage, and will. I had feared that my painful situation was due to too much caring, too much involvement, too much love on my part—for my ex-husband, for the people in my Sardinian field site, and for my profession as a folklorist, which seemed unlikely to yield any kind of permanent employment. I recognized that I was beginning to feel some of the same emotions for my new research subjects and their practices, and I was afraid of screwing up again.

Brigit showed me that love is *necessary* to the processes of understanding and healing: I felt empowered to work with an open heart, in the way that was right for me, as fire would make it whole again. She also forged for me a pen and a knife. To me, these signified my work as an ethnographer, and the processes of writing and analysis it entails. I interpreted them as signs that I was somehow "meant" to continue my research with Pagans, and that I had the goddess's approval and support in doing so. It would be difficult to imagine a stronger message of acceptance and empowerment for me at the time.

I went on to complete that project and write numerous articles, as well as two books, on modern Pagans. It became the central research project of my professional life. In the process, I found new friends in the Pagan community; I found a home. I stayed with Paganism even after my official research had ended: I could say that Brigit was central to my conversion to the craft, if Pagans can truly ever be said to convert.

To this day I can't say for certain whether the goddess Brigit in my vision has an independent existence, or reflected an aspect of my own unconscious, which found expression through Reclaiming's ritual. However, while the intensity of the feelings the vision gave me has diminished over the years, I have never fully lost it. Today, when I lead the guided meditation to the Well of Brigit for my own coven each year at Imbolc, I always bring her the gift of my heart, and she always has a message for me. Last year, the heart I brought her was bursting with red flowers and flames, and the goddess said, "Where I kindled a spark, there is now a bonfire."

REFERENCES:

Alighieri, Dante. 2010. *La Divina Commedia*. Charleston, SC: Nabu Press.

Thomas, Dylan. 1971. *Collected Poems*. New York: W. W. Norton.

In Memoriam: Patricia Monaghan

oon after she submitted the final draft of *Brigit: Sun of Womanhood*, Patricia died at home on November 11th, 2012, in the arms of her husband Michael McDermott after a long journey with cancer. Her loss is devastating to many.

Patricia and Michael worked tirelessly on this anthology throughout her illness. In her email to Goddess Ink with the submittal of the manuscript, Patricia wrote: "This project has been very sustaining during an otherwise very dark time. Thank you for letting us do this."

Michael's words echo what many feel:

She didn't like to be called brave, though she was. She didn't at all like being called a force of nature, but she was. She didn't like it when people said, "How can you do so much?" but she "did" from morn 'till night. We would work hard all day on many things and then say, "Well at least we got a little bit done."

Patricia was a scholar, artist, spiritual practitioner and leader and political activist. She was a gardener and literally a path creator. One of my favorite memories is of her pulling our large honeysuckle bushes in the wet spring soil to create a path in our woods.

This creation she carried into all things, whether leading us to the goddess, to a land ethic or to the struggle for a more just society.

Let us all honor Patricia for all the things she was and will be.

Michael McDermott, editor
Anne Key and Candace Kant, Goddess Ink

THE EDITORS

Michael McDermott is a semi-retired physician and social activist. He has lived at Brigit Rest in Black Earth, Wisconsin for over fifteen years. With his wife, Patricia Monaghan, he provides Brigit Rest as home for the Black Earth Institute (www.blackearthinstitute.org), a progressive think-tank for artists who connect spirituality, social justice, and the environment. In his years as a physician, McDermott worked in the South Bronx at Lincoln Hospital, and for almost thirty years at Cook County Hospital on Chicago's West side. In his work, he sought to identify with the lives of patients, staff, and colleagues in a way that went beyond the technical excellence of medicine. His work included Director of the Adult Emergency Department and founder and leader of the Adult Asthma Clinic, where he still works part time. He also spent time in Nicaragua teaching medicine and helping people in the town of Esteli to plan a health clinic, returning to Chicago to raise money to assist in successfully building the clinic. His devotion to Brigit as an exemplar of bridge-building inspires his life.

Patricia Monaghan (www.patricia-monaghan.com) is the author of the classic *Encyclopedia of Goddesses and Heroines*, the definitive collection of goddess myths from around the world, due out in 2013 in a one-volume paperback edition. She has also written extensively on Irish mythology, including *The Encyclopedia of Celtic Myth and Legend* and *The Red-Haired Girl from the Bog: The Landscape of Irish Myth and Spirit*. A widely published poet, she has four volumes of poetry to her credit, including *Seasons of the Witch* and *Homefront*; the former is a four-part sequence connecting the seasons of a woman's life with the annual solar-lunar cycle; the latter is a meditation on the impact of war on families. Look for her novel in verse, *Mary*, forthcoming from Goddess Ink soon. The poem included in this anthology appears in *Sanctuary*, a collection of poems about the sacredness of land, due from Salmon Publishing in Ireland in March, 2013.

THE CONTRIBUTORS

Aline O'Brien (www.machanightmare.com) has circled with people of diverse Pagan paths throughout the U.S., and in Canada and Brazil. Author of *Witchcraft and the Web* (2001) and *Pagan Pride* (2004), and co-author, with Starhawk, of *The Pagan Book of Living and Dying* (1997), Macha has also contributed to anthologies, periodicals, textbooks, and encyclopedias. A member of the American Academy of Religion, the Marin Interfaith Council, and the Nature Religion Scholars Network, Macha also serves as a national interfaith representative for the Covenant of the Goddess (CoG) and on the advisory board of the Sacred Dying Foundation. Having spent the last eleven years developing and teaching at Cherry Hill Seminary, the first and only seminary serving the Neopagan community, Macha now serves on its board of directors. An all-round Pagan webweaver, she speaks on behalf of Paganism to news media and academic researchers, and lectures at colleges, universities, and seminaries.

Alison Stone's (www.stonepoetry.net) poems have appeared in *The Paris Review, Poetry, Ploughshares, Barrow Street, Poet Lore*, and a variety of other journals and anthologies. She has been awarded Poetry's Frederick Bock Prize and *New York Quarterly's* Madeline Sadin award. Her first book, *They Sing at Midnight*, won the 2003 Many Mountains Moving Poetry Award and was published by Many Mountains Moving Press. A new chapbook, *From the Fool to the World*, written in the voices of the Major Arcana of the tarot, is forthcoming from Parallel Press. She is also a painter and the creator of The Stone Tarot. A licensed psychotherapist, she has private practices in New York City and Nyack.

Annie Finch (www.anniefinch.com) poet, translator, editor, and playwright, has published many books of poetry, including *Calendars, The Encyclopedia of Scotland, Among the Goddesses, and Eve*. Her selected poems, entitled *Spells: New and Selected Poems*, is forthcoming from Wesleyan University Press. Finch's poems have appeared in numerous journals, including: *Yale Review, Kenyon Review, Prairie Schooner, Poetry, Partisan Review,* and *Paris Review*: and in anthologies including *Norton's Anthology of World Poetry* and *The Penguin Anthology of Twentieth-Century American Poetry*. She has also published many anthologies and books about poetry, most recently *A Poet's Craft: A Comprehensive Guide to Making and Sharing Your Poetry* (University of Michigan Press). She writes often about goddesses. She is a senior fellow of Black Earth Institute and directs the Stonecoast low-residency MFA program in Creative Writing at the University of Southern Maine.

Barbara Ardinger (www.barbaraardinger.com) is the author of *Secret Lives*, a new novel about crones and other magical folks, and *Pagan Every Day*, a book of daily meditations. Her other books include *Finding New Goddesses*, a parody of goddess encyclopedias, and an earlier novel, *Quicksilver Moon*, which is realistic . . . except for the vampire. Her day job is freelance editing for people who have good ideas but don't want to embarrass themselves in print. To date, she has edited more than 250 books, both fiction and nonfiction, on a wide range of topics. Barbara, who is well known for the rituals she creates and leads, has also been published in devotionals to Isis and Athena. She holds a PhD in English Renaissance Literature from Southern Illinois University at Carbondale.

Barbara Callan was a musician, songwriter, and moving force in the folkloric and spiritual revival in Connemara, in western County Galway, until her death in early 2001 from cancer, at the age of 52. Her songs exploring and describing women's spiritual journeys have been sung across Ireland. She was the wife of ecologist Dave Hogan and the mother of two boys, Kevin and Brian. An earlier version of this memoir appeared in the American publication, *The Beltane Papers*; a slightly longer version appeared in *Irish Spirit: Pagan, Celtic, Christian, Global*, published in 2001 by Wolfhound Press. Barbara's songs can be heard on the CD, *On the Bright Road*, recorded with harpist Lynn Saoirse (www. lynnsaoirse.com/cd_on_the_bright_road.html).

Barbara Flaherty is the author of two books: *Holy Madness and Doing It Another Way: The Basic Text of the Fourth Order*, both from Chanting Press. Her works have appeared in journals, anthologies, and encyclopediae. A citizen of both the United States and The Republic of Ireland, she was the recipient of the Irish Droghedna Poetry Prize in 2005. She has adapted into English poems of the great Irish/Scottish *bard*, Muireadhach Albanach Ó Dálaigh. Her current poetry project, "Spelling the World," is an exploration of the world as text through the Celtic tradition. Barbara is an interfaith liturgist and has led celebrations of the Celtic feast days annually for up to 300 people. She is the author of *La Morenita: Litany of Our Lady of Guadalupe*, and "The Way of Living Light, A Meditation for Healing through the Consciousness of Christ" (www.christinecenter.org). Barbara is the founding companion of the Fourth Order of Francis and Clare (www.fourthorder.org), a retired chaplain, and dual-diagnosis clinician.

Bee Smith was born in the U.S. and lived twenty years in England before moving with her Irish partner to an acre and a bit in West Cavan, hard by Tuatha dé Danaan country. As well as writing and organic gardening, Bee and her storyteller/musician partner, Tony Cuckson, lead tours through Irish Blessings Tours (www.irishblessingstours.com), guiding groups with an interest in sacred Ireland, fairies, and the goddess around sites in Northwest Ireland and Northern Ireland.

Betz King (www.betzking.com) is a psychologist, writer, teacher, and priestess. She received her PhD in 2006 from The Michigan School of Professional Psychology, where she conducted heuristic, first-person research into women's experiences of embodied spiritual empowerment.

Betz teaches graduate psychology and has a private practice specializing in psycho-spiritual therapy, women's empowerment, and Pagan issues. A spiritual seeker since 1995, Betz is an ordained minister, Reiki Master, Druidic Bard, and a priestess of the Western Mystery Tradition. Betz's approach to spirituality combines feminist theory, Hermetic Qabbalah, Jungian and Transpersonal Psychology, and eclectic earth-based traditions.

Carol P. Christ is descended from an Irish great-grandmother, Elizabeth Ann Kelly, and an Irish great-great-grandmother, Annie Corliss, both of whom raised their children in the tenements of New York City. A founding mother in the field of women and religion, she is author of *She Who Changes, Rebirth of the Goddess, Odyssey with the Goddess, Laughter of Aphrodite, and Diving Deep and Surfacing*, and co-editor of *Womanspirit Rising and Weaving the Visions*. She leads goddess pilgrimages to Crete through Ariadne Institute (www.goddessariadne.org).

Cheryl Straffon is an author, researcher, and editor of writings about ancient sites and the goddess. She is a graduate of London and Cambridge Universities; her published books include *Pagan Cornwall: Land of the Goddess, The Earth Goddess, and Daughters of the Earth*. She lives in Cornwall with her partner, where she edits the magazines *Meyn Mamvro and Goddess Alive!*, and is chair of the Cornish Ancient Sites Protection Network (CASPN). Together with her partner, she also runs Goddess Tours International (www.goddess-tours-international.com), which takes small groups of women to goddess sites in Crete, Malta, Ireland, and the United Kingdom. They both actively celebrate the goddess, including Brigit, around the wheel of the year.

Cindy Thomson (www.cindyswriting.com) is a writer and an avid genealogy enthusiast. Her love of history and her Scots-Irish heritage have inspired much of her writing, including her new Ellis Island series. Cindy is also the author of *Brigid of Ireland* and *Celtic Wisdom: Treasures from Ireland*. She combined her love of history and baseball to co-author the biography *Three Finger: The Mordecai Brown Story*, which was a finalist for the Society for American Baseball Research's Larry Ritter Book Award. In addition to books, Cindy has written on a regular basis for numerous online and print publications and is a mentor for the Jerry B. Jenkins Christian Writers Guild. She is also a member of American Christian Fiction Writers and the Historical Novel Society. Cindy and her husband have three grown sons and live in central Ohio.

Dolores Whelan (www.doloreswhelan.ie) has been involved with education all her adult life, initially as a biochemistry lecturer, and for the past 25 years as an educator and spiritual guide. She holds an MSc in Biochemistry from Trinity College Dublin and an MA in Spirituality. She facilitates workshops and retreats in Celtic spirituality and personal empowerment, and leads pilgrimages to the sacred places in Ireland and Scotland. She is author of *Your Breaking Point*, and a contributor to *Celtic Threads, The Quiet Quarter* ten-year anthology, and *Of Constant Heart*. Her most recent book is *Ever Ancient, Ever New: Celtic Spirituality in 21st Century (2nd Edition)*. A respected speaker at conferences and in the Irish and international media, Dolores believes that the deep truths held within the Celtic spiritual and wisdom tradition is both ancient and new, and is now ready to re-emerge and lead towards a new way for humankind to live in the world. Her work endeavors to support this awakening within the land and people in Ireland, and worldwide.

Elizabeth Cunningham (www.elizabethcunninghamwrites.com) is best known for *The Maeve Chronicles*, a series of award-winning novels featuring the feisty Celtic Magdalen, who is nobody's disciple. An ordained interfaith minister, Cunningham is in private practice as a counselor. She is also the director of the Center at High Valley, where she celebrates the Celtic Cross Quarter Days. She lives in New York State's Hudson Valley.

Emily Stix has a degree in History from the University of Washington. After completing college, she moved to Washington, DC to work as a congressional intern and then an advocate for education in underrepresented communities. Intrigued by the whole-foods and local-foods movements, she worked briefly at a restaurant that emphasized regional foods and wines, before becoming an intern on a sustainable farm in Arizona, where her duties ranged from cleaning and sorting tomatoes to arranging wedding bouquets and selling at farmers' markets. Her dream is to continue working towards bringing sustainable whole foods to ordinary people while continuing her spiritual and personal search.

H. Byron Ballard, BA, MFA (www.myvillagewitch.com), is a ritualist, teacher, speaker, and writer. She has served as a featured speaker and teacher at Sacred Space Conference, Pagan Unity Festival, Southeast Women's Herbal Conference, and other gatherings. Her writings have appeared in print and electronic media. Her essays are featured in several anthologies, including *Birthed from Scorched Hearts* (Fulcrum Press), *Christmas Presence* (Catawba Press), *Women's Voices in Magic* (Megalithica Books), *Into the Great Below*, and *Skalded Apples* (both from Asphodel Press). She blogs as Asheville's Village Witch and as The Village Witch for *Witches and Pagans Magazine*. Her pamphlet, *Back to the Garden: A Handbook for New Pagans*, has been widely distributed, and her first book *Staubs and Ditchwater: An Introduction to Hillfolks Hoodoo* (Silver Rings Press) debuted in June, 2012. Byron is currently at work on *Earth Works: Eight Ceremonies for a Changing Planet*.

Ita Roddy was born in Dublin in 1954 and took a degree in Irish and History at University College Dublin in 1975, followed by an HDip in education in 1976. She taught Irish and history at Notre Dame Secondary School from 1977–2010. Her play, *New York, New York*, was broadcast on RTE Radio, Ireland's national broadcasting service, in 2002; other poems and stories have appeared in various publications. Ita has a passion for the Irish language, culture, and mythology; she is presently working on a short Irish/English book concerning the historical, cultural, and literary wealth of the Irish tradition.

Jill Smith (www.jill-smith.co.uk), artist, writer, and ceremonial performance artist, lives in the Western Isles of Scotland. Having trained as an actress in the early sixties and worked in community art in the early seventies, Jill became a performance artist in the mid-seventies. With her then-husband, she performed large-scale ritual, celebratory ceremonies at fairs and festivals throughout Britain, also working more quietly at ancient sites, the documentation of which appeared in many exhibitions. Following a move from London to Norfolk, Jill became aware of ancient ancestors, spirits of place, and those we may call goddess. She went off into the sacred landscape of Britain on her own, making several major journeys honoring and linking its ancient places. She found herself on the Isle of Lewis in the Western Isles, realized it was her spiritual home, and moved there in 1986. She is author of *The Callanish Dance* (Capall Bann 2000) and *Mother of the Isles* (Dor Dama Press 2003).

Jude Lally (www.celticsoulcraft.com) is from the West Coast of Scotland, but in 2009 she relocated to the Blue Ridge Mountains of Asheville, North Carolina. She received an MSc with the University of Strathclyde in Human Ecology, undertaking her thesis study on the Celtic goddess Brigit and exploring her relevance to cultural activists in contemporary Scotland. She presented at the Interaction with the Sacred from Devotion to Divination conference at Edinburgh University in 2009. The move to the United States facilitated an exploration of fiber art, inspired by its ancient heritage; this then flourished into a practice of creative spirituality. An ecofeminist and human ecologist, her workshops honor the cycle of the year inspired by Celtic spirituality, blending creative expression while facilitating a connection to the sacred. Her work explores the roots of fostering a new consciousness rooted in ancient spiritual bedrock. She works with survivors of interpersonal violence to create empowering responses to social crisis. She is a member of the Centre for Human Ecology in Scotland and The Mother Grove Temple in Asheville.

Joan McBreen (www.joanmcbreen.com) divides her time between Tuam and Renvyle, County Galway, Ireland. She has published four collections of poetry and has edited two anthologies, including the significant anthology of Irish women's poetry, *The White Page*. Her most recent books are *Heather Island* and *The Watchful Heart: A New Generation of Irish Poets*. A new collection of poetry is due from Salmon Poetry in 2013.

Kerry Noonan has a PhD in Folklore and Mythology from UCLA, for which she focused on women's vernacular religious beliefs and practices, as well as Celtic folklore. She is now a college professor in Vermont. Her writings on Dianic Witchcraft, Wicca, Catholic Charismatic women, and the Haitian lwa Grande Brigitte can be found in various scholarly publications. Kerry has been active in the goddess movement for 24 years, is an ordained priestess in the Dianic tradition, and has served in that capacity for Circle of Aradia, Temple of Diana, and Sisters of the Moon, teaching and facilitating rituals. She has been devoted to Brigit for many years.

Kersten Christianson is a raven-watching, moon-gazing Alaskan who teaches high school English (including mythology) and French, and composes poetry in the Tongass Forest of south east Alaska. She has taught in various schools throughout the state, including schools on the Kenai Peninsula, St. Lawrence Island, and the North Slope, before returning home to teach at Sitka by the Sea. She lives with her partner Bruce, free-spirited daughter Rie, and yellow lab Odin. Summers are spent traveling and tent camping in northern destinations and across Canada. Kersten is also the co-editor of the quarterly journal, *Alaska Women Speak* (http://alaskawomenspeak.org), a journal with a statewide presence devoted to publishing the words and experiences of Alaskan women. Kersten's poetry has been published in *Alaskan Women Speak, Tidal Echoes,* and *We'Moon.*

Kirsten Brunsgaard Clausen (kirsten.brunsgaard@gmail.com) lives in Stockholm, Sweden. A skilled weaver for almost thirty years, she is also a storyteller and writes of the original goddesses and wise mothers of old Scandinavia: Braido, Omma, Källingen, and Hel. Kirsten has undertaken long-term university studies in theology and latterly in thealogy*. She also works as a psychosomatic physiotherapist, intertwining body, soul, feelings, and intellect. Kirsten deeply enjoys women connecting with one another, drawing up threads from our peaceful, life-oriented history of

---

* Editor's Note: The subject of "theology" is God, and of "thealogy," Goddess.

old to make a strong web for the future. She has organized four Swedish Goddess Conferences.

Mael Brigde lives in Vancouver, Canada. She is the founder of the Daughters of the Flame, who have been tending Brigit's flame since Imbolc, 1993. She is currently working on a book of poems and prayers to Brigit. Mael Brigde keeps a list of Brigit-related books on LibraryThing (www.librarything.com/catalog/MaelBrigde) as well as maintaining *Brigit's Sparkling Flame* (http://brigitssparklingflame. blogspot.com/), a blog with posts on books, events, art, people, websites, and anything else with links to Brigit that catches her eye.

Matthew Geden was born in England and moved to Kinsale, Ireland, where he runs a bookstore, in 1990. He cofounded the SoundEye International Poetry Festival. His poems have appeared in several publications at home and abroad, including *Something Beginning with P, Poets of the Millennium, The Backyards of Heaven* and *Landing Places: Immigrant Poets in Ireland*. His first full-length collection, *Swimming to Albania*, was published by Bradshaw Books in 2009.

Miriam Robbins Dexter holds a PhD in Indo-European Studies (comparative linguistics, ancient Indo-European languages, archaeology, and comparative mythology) from UCLA. Her first book, *Whence the Goddesses: A Source Book*, was used for courses she taught at UCLA for a decade and a half. Her latest book, *Sacred Display: Divine and Magical Female Figures of Eurasia*, co-authored with Victor Mair, recently won the Sarasvati Award from the Association for Study of Women and Mythology (ASWM) for best nonfiction book on women and mythology. Miriam is the author of over twenty scholarly articles and nine encyclopedia articles on ancient female figures. She has edited and co-edited sixteen scholarly volumes. She currently co-edits conference proceedings for the Institute of Archaeomythology. For thirteen years, she taught courses in Latin, Greek, and Sanskrit languages in the department of Classics at USC. She has lectured at the New Bulgarian University and Alexandru Ioan Cuza University (Romania).

Phoenix LeFae (www.phoenixlefae.com) is an eclectic witch who has been intertwined with the Reclaiming community for over fifteen years. A lover of the liminal spaces—all that is and isn't—Phoenix is a child of paradox. She is a professional priestess and writer, using magic and words to create new worlds and change the mundane one. Phoenix can often be found dancing through the multiverses, all the while immersed in conversation with deity, animal spirits, and the fae (faeries, pixies, gnomes, and other beings). She believes that magic and ritual can transform lives, and she works to prove that every day. Tarot reader, belly dancer, mother, wife, sister, and friend, Phoenix lives to live outside of her labels.

Ruth Barrett (www.dancingtreemusic.com) is a Dianic high priestess, ritualist, educator, author of *Women's Rites, Women's Mysteries: Intuitive Ritual Creation*, and award-winning recording artist of original goddess songs. Ruth's numerous recordings, beginning in 1980, have been among the pioneering musical works in the goddess spirituality movement. She is known for her dulcimer artistry; her original folk music, inspired by folklore, goddess mythology, and celebration of nature; and her arrangements of traditional Celtic and English folk music.

Sabina Magliocco is Professor of Anthropology at California State University, Northridge. She grew up in Italy and the United States. She received her AB from Brown University in 1980 and her PhD from Indiana University in 1988. A recipient of Guggenheim, National Endowment for the Humanities, Fulbright, and Hewlett fellowships, and an honorary Fellow of the American Folklore Society, she has published on religion, folklore, food ways, festival, and witchcraft in Europe and the United States, and is a leading authority on the modern Pagan movement. She is the author of numerous books and articles, including *Witching Culture: Folklore* and *Neo-Paganism in America* (2004) and *Neopagan Sacred Art & Altars: Making Things Whole* (2001); produced the documentary film series, *Oss Tales*, with filmmaker John M. Bishop, on a May Day custom in Cornwall and its reclamation by American Pagans. A Gardnerian priestess with Reclaiming training, she has an eclectic coven in the Los Angeles area.

Slippery Elm (www.freestylegrove.com) is a witch, poet, and hip-hop emcee from Vancouver, Canada. He performs his poetry in the street and at venues, festivals, and political actions across the Pacific Northwest. He is a member of Brigid's Irregulars, and explores *filidecht*, the ancient Irish tradition of seer-poets. Most recently, his work has appeared in *Mandragora: Further Explorations in Esoteric Poesies*. He is a permaculture activist and strives to support garden initiatives and green urban areas wherever he goes. As a member of jazz/hip-hop trio Elekwent Folk, he has released five albums; *Nazza*, his first book of poetry, was published in 2011 on the summer solstice. He haunts bookstores and wild places.

Stuart McHardy is a teller of tales, singer of songs, lecturer in Scottish history and folklore, and author of many books, including *The Quest for the Nine Maidens* and the recent *Pagan Symbols of the Picts*. Having been published as a poet since the seventies, he has held such diverse positions as Director of the Scots Language Centre and President of the Pictish Arts Society. Originally from Dundee, he lives in central Edinburgh with his wife, Sandra, but travels all over Scotland appearing at festivals, in schools, and speaking to various groups and societies; whenever possible, he wanders the hills. He is currently part of a group studying the history and influence of the Corryvreckan whirlpool, associated with the *cailleach*, Scotland's oldest known mythical being and original mother goddess.

Szmeralda Shanel is an ordained priestess of Isis/Auset with the Fellowship of Isis and the Temple of Isis. She is an initiate in the Anderson Feri tradition and the founder of the Iseum of Black Isis (www.blackisisiseum.com), an iseum dedicated to goddess spirituality and sacred arts. Outside the circle, Szmeralda Shanel makes ends meet working as a teaching artist, expressive arts therapist, and a tarot reader.

Valerie Freseman is a priestess of Brigit and has been the High Priestess of Strangers' Gate Coven since 2001. She holds clergy credentials through the Covenant of the Goddess and is currently pursuing her MDiv at Union

Theological Seminary in New York. She is the local co-coordinator of New York City Pagan Pride, and enjoys engaging in thinking about how the Neopagan religious movement contributes to the world religious landscape on questions of theology, ethics, and altruism, and inter-faith. She blogs on her spirituality and her thoughts on activism, ministry, poetry, magic, and other topics at Sparks Upon the Water (www.sparksuwponthewater.wordpress.com).

Acknowledgments

The publishers would like to acknowledge all of those that have helped bring this book to fruition. First, thanks go to Soujanya Rao, whose artistic sensibilities matched with technical skill bring beautiful and readable formatting to this publication. Heartfelt thanks go to Lynne Melcombe (www.lynnemelcombe.com) for attentive copy editing and proofreading and her patience with the ever changing production schedule. Thanks to Katlyn Breene (www.mermadearts.com) for the front cover art and Eric Koenig for the back cover art.

CPSIA information can be obtained at www.ICGtesting.com
Printed in the USA
LVOW13s1219060813

346538LV00004B/7/P